THE BEST OF LUDWIG VON MISES

LUDWIG VON MISES

AMERICAN INSTITUTE FOR ECONOMIC RESEARCH

The Best of Ludwig von Mises
By Ludwig von Mises
Edited with a Foreword by Jeffrey Tucker

ISBN 978-1-63-069182-0

Cover design: Vanessa Mendozzi

THE BEST OF LUDWIG VON MISES

LUDWIG VON MISES

AIER | AMERICAN INSTITUTE *for* ECONOMIC RESEARCH

Contents

FOREWORD

It's a seemingly impossible task to select the "best" of Ludwig von Mises (1881-1973) whose teaching and writing career spanned six decades and whose literary output includes several mighty and timeless treatises on political economy. They were not written in isolation from the real and often horrifying events of the 20th century; they were heavily informed by the brilliance and tragedy of his life experiences – including as a refugee forced to flee his home in Vienna – in battling every form of totalitarianism. I've been reading his work since the dawn of my intellectual consciousness but I've yet to discover the end of his capacity to illuminate the world around us. I never fail to profit from re-reading even the books I think I understand best. Learning from Mises is a lifelong project.

And yet, there is a need for this book. The pieces herein are selected for their unusual intellectual power even within the Misesian milieu. They neglect many areas such as his extensive work on the methodology of the social sciences, the operation of the business cycle, the theory of money and credit, his distinct theory of capital and interest, and his writings on European history and philosophy, among a thousand other areas. But they are chosen because they well illustrate what are the most prescient and pertinent ideas that are needed in our time, and maybe all times.

We begin with the sweeping history of the rise of modernity through the gradual emancipation of the world through the ideas of freedom. *Liberty and Property* was delivered in 1956 as a reminder of the stakes of the great intellectual debates. The choice of freedom over control makes the difference between a life of dignity and opportunity over degradation and suffering. In *Liberty and Property*, Mises identifies the crucial difference that capitalism made: it shifted the locus of control from the elites to the common person, thereby unleashing human creativity and massively raising living standards for everyone.

The second essay, *Planned Chaos*, was written after Mises was settled in the U.S., following his 6 years in Geneva (he immigrated in 1940), and it recounts the rise of socialism and fascism in Europe. It presents in the briefest possible way the intellectual origins of totalitarianism and contrasts this with freedom and free markets. This essay is painful in so many ways, once the reader realizes that this man lived through all the history he recounts here. Some insights concern the horrors of Nazism he might have been responsible for bringing to print, such as the relationship between eugenics as practiced in the U.S. and Nazi methods of demographic planning that ended in mass murder. This essay is far too often overlooked, even by Misesians.

Profit and Loss is Mises's clearest and briefest discussion of the centrality of the price system in enabling commercial function. Profit and loss are the signs and symbols of rational resource allocation, not even slightly dispensable for wealth creation and a functioning social order. Understanding this essay helps the reader see what's really behind business functioning and its purpose in economic life. It's almost a guarantee that anyone who inveighs against free enterprise or otherwise wants to supplant competition with regulation is completely unaware of the social function of prices.

Next comes the earliest piece from 1920, "Economic Calculation in the Socialist Commonwealth." In the broader economics profession, it is the best-known essay of his career. It claimed, at the very dawn of the Soviet socialist experiment, that socialism is impossible – not in the sense that it could not be tried but in the sense that socialism is utterly incompatible with economics both in theory and practice. So, he predicted, it would only produce failure. It was a conclusion that almost the whole of European intellectual culture was prepared to reject. Mises made that very difficult because his explanation was so complete.

We end finally with a short excerpt from my personal favorite of Mises's books, *Liberalism*, from 1927. The period in which he was writing is telling. The old liberalism was dying, he knew, but he wanted to write one lasting manifesto in which he could speak for liberalism as an idea. It was one last restatement before socialism and fascism swept the civilized world. The book patiently presents all the ideas chapter by chapter: trade, property, association, peace, markets, tolerance, self-determination. As he approaches the end, he gives the reader a standard by which to measure genuinely liberal movements. They rely not on manipulating the senses of the public but rather on the appeal to reason. Not through mass rallies, uniforms, strong leaders, and public agitation will we win but through sound arguments.

Thus ends *The Best of Mises* – the end of this book but, we can hope, not the end of the journey through the work of this brilliant thinker whose ideas belong to the ages and to us all.

Jeffrey Tucker
American Institute for Economic Research

LIBERTY AND PROPERTY

Ludwig von Mises presented "Liberty and Property" as a talk at the opening session of the Mont Pelerin Society meeting in Princeton, N.J., September 8, 1958.

1.

At the end of the eighteenth century there prevailed two notions of liberty, each of them very different from what we have in mind today referring to liberty and freedom. The first of these conceptions was purely academic and without any application to the conduct of political affairs. It was an idea derived from the books of the ancient authors, the study of which was then the sum and substance of higher education. In the eyes of these Greek and Roman writers, freedom was not something that had to be granted to all men. It was a privilege of the minority, to be withheld from the majority. What the Greeks called democracy was, in the light of present-day terminology, not what Lincoln called government by the people, but oligarchy, the sovereignty of full-right citizens in a community in which the masses were meteques or slaves. Even this rather limited freedom after the fourth century before Christ was not dealt with by the philosophers, historians, and orators as a practical constitutional institution. As they saw it, it was a feature of the past irretrievably lost. They bemoaned the passing of this golden age, but they did not know any method of returning to it.

The second notion of liberty was no less oligarchic, although it was not inspired by any literary reminiscences. It was the ambition of the landed aristocracy, and sometimes also of urban patricians, to preserve their privileges against the rising power of royal absolutism. In most parts of continental Europe, the princes remained victorious in these conflicts. Only in England and in the Netherlands did the gentry and the urban patricians succeed in defeating the dynasties. But what they won was not freedom for all, but only freedom for an elite, for a minority of the people.

We must not condemn as hypocrites the men who in those ages praised liberty, while they preserved the legal disabilities of the many, even serfdom and slavery. They were faced with a problem which they did not know how to solve satisfactorily. The traditional system of production was too narrow for a continually rising population. The number of people for whom there was, in a full sense of the term, no room left by the pre-capitalistic methods of agriculture and artisanship was increasing. These supernumeraries were starving paupers. They were a menace to the preservation of the existing order of society and, for a long time, nobody could think of another order, a state of affairs, that would feed all of these poor wretches. There could not be any question of granting them full civil rights, still less of giving them a share of the conduct of affairs of state. The only expedient the rulers knew was to keep them quiet by resorting to force.

2.

The pre-capitalistic system of product(ion) was restrictive. Its historical basis was military conquest. The victorious kings had given the land to their paladins. These aristocrats were lords in the literal meaning of the word, as they did not depend on the patronage of consumers buying or abstaining from buying on a market. On the other hand, they themselves were the main customers of the processing industries which, under the guild system, were organized on a corporative scheme. This scheme was opposed to innovation. It forbade deviation from the traditional methods of production. The number of people for whom there were jobs even in agriculture or in the arts and crafts was limited. Under these conditions, many a man, to use the words of Malthus, had to discover that "at nature's mighty feast there is no vacant cover for him," and that "she tells him to be gone."[1] But some of these outcasts nevertheless managed to survive, begot children, and made the number of destitute grow hopelessly more and more.

But then came capitalism. It is customary to see the radical innovations that capitalism brought about in the substitution of the mechanical factory for the more primitive and less efficient methods of the artisans' shops. This is a rather superficial view. The characteristic feature of capitalism that distinguishes it from pre-capitalist methods of production was its new principle of marketing. Capitalism is not simply mass production, but mass production to satisfy the needs of the masses. The arts and crafts of the good old days had catered almost exclusively to the wants of the well-to-do. But the factories produced cheap goods for the many. All the early factories turned out was designed to serve the masses, the same strata that worked in the factories. They served them either by supplying them directly or indirectly by exporting and thus providing for them foreign food and raw materials. This principle of marketing was the signature of early capitalism as it is of present-day capitalism. The employees themselves are the customers consuming the much greater part of all goods produced. They are the sovereign customers who are "always right." Their

---

1 Thomas R. Malthus, *An Essay on the Principle of Population*, 2nd ed. (London, 1803), p. 531.

buying or abstention from buying determines what has to be produced, in what quantity, and of what quality. In buying what suits them best they make some enterprises profit and expand and make other enterprises lose money and shrink. Thereby they are continually shifting control of the factors of production into the hands of those businessmen who are most successful in filling their wants. Under capitalism private property of the factors of production is a social function. The entrepreneurs, capitalists, and land owners are mandataries, as it were, of the consumers, and their mandate is revocable. In order to be rich, it is not sufficient to have once saved and accumulated capital. It is necessary to invest it again and again in those lines in which it best fills the wants of the consumers. The market process is a daily repeated plebiscite, and it ejects inevitably from the ranks of profitable people those who do not employ their property according to the orders given by the public. But business, the target of fanatical hatred on the part of all contemporary governments and self-styled intellectuals, acquires and preserves bigness only because it works for the masses. The plants that cater to the luxuries of the few never attain big size. The shortcoming of nineteenth-century historians and politicians was that they failed to realize that the workers were the main consumers of the products of industry. In their view, the wage earner was a man toiling for the sole benefit of a parasitic leisure class. They labored under the delusion that the factories had impaired the lot of the manual workers. If they had paid any attention to statistics they would easily have discovered the fallaciousness of their opinion. Infant mortality dropped, the average length of life was prolonged, the population multiplied, and the average common man enjoyed amenities of which even the well-to-do of earlier ages did not dream.

However this unprecedented enrichment of the masses were merely a by-product of the Industrial Revolution. Its main achievement was the transfer of economic supremacy from the owners of land to the totality of the population. The common man was no longer a drudge who had to be satisfied with the crumbs that fell from the tables of the rich. The three pariah castes which were characteristic of the pre-capitalistic ages—the slaves, the serfs, and those people whom patristic and scholastic authors as well as British legislation from the sixteenth to the nineteenth centuries referred to as the poor—disappeared. Their scions became, in this new setting of business, not only free workers, but also customers. This radical change was reflected in the emphasis laid by business on markets. What business needs first of all is markets and again markets. This was the watchword of capitalistic enterprise. Markets, that means patrons, buyers, consumers. There is under capitalism one way to wealth: to serve the consumers better and cheaper than other people do.

Within the shop and factory the owner — or in the corporations, the representative of the shareholders, the president — is the boss. But this mastership is merely apparent and conditional. It is subject to the supremacy of the consumers. The consumer is king, is the real boss, and the manufacturer is done for if he does not outstrip his competitors in best serving consumers.

It was this great economic transformation that changed the face of the world. It very soon transferred political power from the hands of a privileged minority into the hands of the people. Adult franchise followed in the wake of industrial enfranchisement. The common man, to whom the market process had given the power to choose the entrepreneur and capitalists, acquired the analogous power in the field of government. He became a voter.

It has been observed by eminent economists, I think first by the late Frank A. Fetter, that the market is a democracy in which every penny gives a right to vote. It would be more correct to say that representative government by the people is an attempt to arrange constitutional affairs according to the model of the market, but this design can never be fully achieved. In the political field it is always the will of the majority that prevails, and the minorities must yield to it. It serves also minorities, provided they are not so insignificant in number as to become negligible. The garment industry produces clothes not only for normal people, but also for the stout, and the publishing trade publishes not only westerns and detective stories for the crowd, but also books for discriminating readers. There is a second important difference. In the political sphere, there is no means for an individual or a small group of individuals to disobey the will of the majority. But in the intellectual field private property makes rebellion possible. The rebel has to pay a price for his independence; there are in this universe no prizes that can be won without sacrifices. But if a man is willing to pay the price, he is free to deviate from the ruling orthodoxy or neo-orthodoxy. What would conditions have been in the socialist commonwealth for heretics like Kierkegaard, Schopenhauer, Veblen, or Freud? For Monet, Courbet, Walt Whitman, Rilke, or Kafka? In all ages, pioneers of new ways of thinking and acting could work only because private property made contempt of the majority's ways possible. Only a few of these separatists were themselves economically independent enough to defy the government into the opinions of the majority.

But they found in the climate of the free economy among the public people prepared to aid and support them. What would Marx have done without his patron, the manufacturer Friedrich Engels?

3.

What vitiates entirely the socialists' economic critique of capitalism is their failure to grasp the sovereignty of the consumers in the market economy. They see only hierarchical organization of the various enterprises and plans, and are at a loss to realize that the profit system forces business to serve the consumers. In their dealings with their employers, the unions proceed as if only malice and greed were to prevent what they call management from paying higher wage rates. Their shortsightedness does not see anything beyond the doors of the factory. They and their henchmen talk about the concentration of economic power, and do not realize that economic power is ultimately vested in the hands of the buying public of which the employees themselves form the immense majority. Their inability to comprehend things as they are is reflected in such inappropriate metaphors as industrial kingdom and dukedoms. They are too dull to see the difference between a sovereign king or duke who could be dispossessed only by a more powerful conqueror and a "chocolate king" who forfeits his "kingdom" as soon as the customers prefer to patronize another supplier. This distortion is at the bottom of all socialist plans. If any of the socialist chiefs had tried to earn his living by selling hot dogs, he would have learned something about the sovereignty of the customers. But they were professional revolutionaries and their only job was to kindle civil war. Lenin's ideal was to build a nation's production effort according to the model of the post office, an outfit that does not depend on the consumers, because its deficits are covered by compulsory collection of taxes. "The whole of society," he said, was to "become one office and one factory."[2]

He did not see that the very character of the office and the factory is entirely changed when it is alone in the world and no longer grants to people the opportunity to choose among the products and services of various enterprises. Because his blindness made it impossible for him to see the role the market and the consumers play under capitalism, he could not see the difference between freedom and slavery. Because in his eyes the workers were only workers and not also customers, he believed they were already slaves under capitalism, and that one did not change their status when nationalizing all plants and shops. Socialism substitutes the sovereignty of a dictator, or committee of dictators, for the sovereignty of the consumers. Along with the economic sovereignty of the citizens disappears also their political sovereignty. To the unique production plan that annuls any planning on the part of the consumers corresponds in the constitutional sphere the one party principle that deprives the citizens of any opportunity to plan the course of public affairs. Freedom is indivisible. He who has not the faculty to choose among various brands of canned food or soap, is also deprived of the power to choose between various political parties and programs and to elect

2 V.I. Lenin, *State and Revolution* (New York: International Publishers, s.d.) p. 84.

the officeholders. He is no longer a man; he becomes a pawn in the hands of the supreme social engineer. Even his freedom to rear progeny will be taken away by eugenics. Of course, the socialist leaders occasionally assure us that dictatorial tyranny is to last only for the period of transition from capitalism and representative government to the socialist millennium in which everybody's wants and wishes will be fully satisfied.[3] Once the socialist regime is "sufficiently secure to risk criticism," Miss Joan Robinson, the eminent representative of the British neo-Cambridge school, is kind enough to promise us, "even independent philharmonic societies" will be allowed to exist.[4] Thus the liquidation of all dissenters is the condition that will bring us what the communists call freedom. From this point of view we may also understand what another distinguished Englishman, Mr. J.G. Crowther, had in mind when he praised inquisition as "beneficial to science when it protects a rising class."[5] The meaning of all this is clear. When all people meekly bow to a dictator, there will no longer be any dissenters left for liquidation. Caligula, Torquemada, Robespierre would have agreed with this solution.

The socialists have engineered a semantic revolution in converting the meaning of terms into their opposite. In the vocabulary of their "newspeak," as George Orwell called it,

---

3 Karl Marx, *Zur Kritik des Sozialdemoskratischen Programms von Gotha*, ed. Kreibich (Reichenberg, 1920), p. 23.

4 Joan Robinson, *Private Enterprise and Public Control* (published for the Association for education in Citzenship by the English Universities Press, Ltd., s.d.), pp. 13–14.

5 J.G. Crowther, *Social Relations of Science* (London, 1941), p. 333.

there is a term "the one-party principle." Now etymologically party is derived from the noun part. The brotherless part is no longer different from its antonym, the whole; it is identical with it. A brotherless party is not a party, and the one party principle is in fact a no-party principle. It is a suppression of any kind of opposition. Freedom implies the right to choose between assent and dissent. But in newspeak it means the duty to assent unconditionally and strict interdiction of dissent. This reversal of the traditional connotation of all words of the political terminology is not merely a peculiarity of the language of the Russian Communists and their Fascist and Nazi disciples. The social order that in abolishing private property deprives the consumers of their autonomy and independence, and thereby subjects every man to the arbitrary discretion of the central planning board, could not win the support of the masses if they were not to camouflage its main character. The socialists would have never duped the voters if they had openly told them that their ultimate end is to cast them into bondage. For exoteric use they were forced to pay lip-service to the traditional appreciation of liberty.

4.

It was different in the esoteric discussions among the inner circles of the great conspiracy. There the initiated did not dissemble their intentions concerning liberty. Liberty was, in their opinion, certainly a good feature in the past in the frame of bourgeois society because it provided them with the opportunity to embark on their schemes. But once socialism has triumphed, there is no longer any need for free thought and autonomous action on the part of individuals. Any further change can only be a deviation from the perfect state that mankind has attained in reaching the bliss of socialism. Under such conditions, it would be simply lunacy to tolerate dissent.

Liberty, says the Bolshevist, is a bourgeois prejudice. The common man does not have any ideas of his own, he does not write books, does not hatch heresies, and does not invent new methods of production. He just wants to enjoy life. He has no use for the class interests of the intellectuals who make a living as professional dissenters and innovators.

This is certainly the most arrogant disdain of the plain citizen ever devised. There is no need to argue this point. For the question is not whether or not the common man can himself take advantage of the liberty to think, to speak, and to write books. The question is whether or not the sluggish routinist profits from the freedom granted to those who eclipse him in intelligence and will power. The common man may look with indifference and even contempt upon the dealings of better people. But he is delighted to enjoy all the benefits which the endeavors of the innovators put at his disposal. He has no comprehension of what in his eyes is merely inane hair-splitting. But as soon as these thoughts and theories are utilized by enterprising businessmen for satisfying some of his latent wishes, he hurries to acquire the new products. The common man is without doubt the main beneficiary of all the accomplishments of modern science and technology.

It is true, a man of average intellectual abilities has no chance to rise to the rank of a captain of industry. But the sovereignty that the market assigns to him in economic affairs stimulates technologists and promoters to convert to his use all the achievements of scientific research. Only people whose intellectual horizon does not extend beyond the internal organization of the factory and who do not realize what makes the businessmen run, fail to notice this fact.

The admirers of the Soviet system tell us again and again that freedom is not the supreme good. It is "not worth having," if it implies poverty. To sacrifice it in order to attain wealth for the masses, is in their eyes fully justified. But for a few unruly individualists who cannot adjust themselves to the ways of regular fellows, all people in Russia are perfectly happy. We may leave it undecided whether this happiness was also shared by the millions of Ukrainian peasants who died from starvation, by the inmates of the forced labor camps, and by the Marxian leaders who were purged. But we cannot pass over the fact that the standard of living was incomparably higher in the free countries of the West than in the communist east. In giving away liberty as the price to be paid for the acquisition of prosperity, the Russians made a poor bargain. They now have neither the one nor the other.

5.

Romantic philosophy labored under the illusion that in the early ages of history the individual was free and that the course of historical evolution deprived him of his primordial liberty. As Jean-Jacques Rousseau saw it, nature accorded men freedom and society enslaved him. In fact, primeval man was at the mercy of every fellow who was stronger and therefore could snatch away from him the scarce means of subsistence. There is in nature nothing to which the name of liberty could be given. The concept of freedom always refers to social relations between men. True, society cannot realize the illusory concept of the individual's absolute independence. Within society everyone depends on what other people are prepared to contribute to his well-being in return for his own contribution to their well-being. Society is essentially the mutual exchange of services. As far as individuals have the opportunity to choose, they are free; if they are forced by violence or threat of violence to surrender to the terms of an exchange, no matter how they feel about it, they lack freedom. This slave is unfree precisely because the master assigns him his tasks and determines what he has to receive if he fulfills it.

As regards the social apparatus of repression and coercion, the government, there cannot be any question of freedom. Government is essentially the negation of liberty. It is the recourse to violence or threat of violence in order to make all people obey the orders of the government, whether they like it or not. As far as the government's jurisdiction extends, there is coercion, not freedom. Government is a necessary institution, the means to make the social system of cooperation work smoothly without being disturbed by violent acts on the part of gangsters whether of domestic or of foreign origin. Government is not, as some people like to say, a necessary evil; it is not an evil, but a means, the only means available to make peaceful human coexistence possible. But it is the opposite of liberty. It is beating, imprisoning, hanging. Whatever a government does it is ultimately supported by the actions of armed constables. If the government operates a school or a hospital, the funds required are collected by taxes, i.e., by payments exacted from the citizens.

If we take into account the fact that, as human nature is, there can neither be civilization nor peace without the functioning of the government apparatus of violent action, we may call government the most beneficial human institution. But the fact remains that government is repression not freedom. Freedom is to be found only in the sphere in which government does not interfere. Liberty is always freedom from the government. It is the restriction of the government's interference. It prevails only in the fields in which the citizens have the opportunity to choose the way in which they want to proceed. Civil rights are the statutes that precisely circumscribe the sphere in which the men conducting the affairs of state are permitted to restrict the individuals' freedom to act.

The ultimate end that men aim at by establishing government is to make possible the operation of a definite system of social cooperation under the principle of the division of labor. If the social system which people want to have is socialism (communism, planning) there is no sphere of freedom left. All citizens are in every regard subject to orders of the government. The state is a total state; the regime is totalitarian. The government alone plans and forces everybody to behave according with this unique plan. In the market economy the individuals are free to choose the way in which they want to integrate themselves into the frame of social cooperation. As far as the sphere of market exchange extends, there is spontaneous action on the part of individuals. Under this system that is called laissez-faire, and which Ferdinand Lassalle dubbed as the night-watchman state, there is freedom because there is a field in which individuals are free to plan for themselves.

The socialists must admit there cannot be any freedom under a socialist system. But they try to obliterate the difference between the servile state and economic freedom by denying that there is any freedom in the mutual exchange of commodities and services on the market. Every market exchange is, in the words of a school of pro-socialist lawyers, "a coercion over other people's liberty." There is, in their eyes, no difference worth mentioning between a man's paying a tax or a fine imposed by a magistrate, or his buying a newspaper or admission to a movie. In each of these cases the man is subject to governing power. He's not free, for, as professor Hale says, a man's freedom means "the absence of any obstacle to his use of material goods."[6] This means: I am not free, because a woman who has knitted a sweater, perhaps as a birthday present for her husband, puts an obstacle to my using it. I myself am restricting all other people's freedom because I object to their using my toothbrush. In doing this I am, according to this doctrine, exercising private governing power, which is analogous to public government power, the powers that the government exercises in imprisoning a man in Sing Sing.

Those expounding this amazing doctrine consistently conclude that liberty is nowhere to be found. They assert that what they call economic pressures do not essentially differ from the pressures the masters practice with regard to their slaves. They reject what they call private governmental power, but they don't object to the restriction of liberty by public government power. They want to

---

6 Robert L. Hale, *Freedom Through Law: Public Control of Private Governing Power* (New York: Columbia University, 1952), pp. 4 ff.

concentrate all what they call restrictions of liberty in the hands of the government. They attack the institution of private property and the laws that, as they say, stand "ready to enforce property rights—that is, to deny liberty to anyone to act in a way which violates them."[7]

A generation ago all housewives prepared soup by proceeding in accordance with the recipes that they had got from their mothers or from a cookbook. Today many housewives prefer to buy a canned soup, to warm it and to serve it to their family. But, say our learned doctors, the canning corporation is in a position to restrict the housewife's freedom because, in asking a price for the tin can, it puts an obstacle to her use of it. People who did not enjoy the privilege of being tutored by these eminent teachers, would say that the canned product was turned out by the cannery, and that the corporation in producing it removed the greatest obstacle to a consumer's getting and using a can, viz., its nonexistence. The mere essence of a product cannot gratify anybody without its existence. But they are wrong, say the doctors. The corporation dominates the housewife, it destroys by its excessive concentrated power over her individual freedom, and it is the duty of the government to prevent such a gross offense. Corporations, say, under the auspices of the Ford Foundation, another of this group, Professor Berle, must be subjected to the control of the government.[8]

7 Ibid., p. 5.

8 A.A. Berle, Jr., *Economic Power and the Free Society, a Preliminary Discussion of the Corporation* (New York: the Fund for the Republic, 1954).

Why does our housewife buy the canned product rather than cling to the methods of her mother and grandmother? No doubt because she thinks this way of acting is more advantageous for her than the traditional custom. Nobody forced her. There were people—they are called jobbers, promoters, capitalists, speculators, stock exchange gamblers—who had the idea of satisfying a latent wish of millions of housewives by investing in the cannery industry. And there are other equally selfish capitalists who, in many hundreds of other corporations, provide consumers with many hundreds of other things. The better a corporation serves the public, the more customers it gets, the bigger it grows. Go into the home of the average American family and you will see for whom the wheels of the machines are turning.

In a free country nobody is prevented from acquiring riches by serving the consumers better than they are served already. What he needs is only brains and hard work. "Modern civilization, nearly all civilization," said Edwin Cannan, the last in a long line of eminent British economists, "is based on the principle of making things pleasant for those who please the market, and unpleasant for those who fail to do so."[9] All this talk about the concentration of economic power is vain. The bigger a corporation is, the more people it serves, the more does it depend on pleasing the consumers, the many, the masses. Economic power, in the market economy, is in the hands of the consumers.

Capitalistic business is not perseverance in the once attained state of production. It is rather ceaseless innovation, daily repeated

9 Edwin Cannan, *An Economist's Protest* (London, 1928), pp. vi ff.

attempts to improve the provision of the consumers by new, better and cheaper products. Any actual state of production activities is merely transitory. There prevails incessantly the tendency to supplant what is already achieved by something that serves the consumers better. There is consequently under capitalism a continuous circulation of elites. What characterizes the men whom one calls the captains of industry is the ability to contribute new ideas and to put them to work. However big a corporation must be, it is doomed as soon as it does not succeed in adjusting itself daily anew to the best possible methods of serving the consumers. But the politicians and other would-be reformers see only the structure of industry as its exists today. They think that they are clever enough to snatch from business control of the plants as they are today, and to manage them by sticking to already established routines. While the ambitious newcomer, who will be the tycoon of tomorrow, is already preparing plans for things unheard of before, all they have in mind is to conduct affairs along tracks already beaten. There is no record of an industrial innovation contrived and put into practice by bureaucrats. If one does not want to plunge into stagnation, a free hand must be left to those today unknown men who have the ingenuity to lead mankind forward on the way to more and more satisfactory conditions. This is the main problem of a nation's economic organization.

Private property of the material factors of production is not a restriction of the freedom of all other people to choose what suits them best. It is, on the contrary, the means that assigns to the common man, in his capacity as a buyer, supremacy in all economic affairs. It is the means to stimulate a nation's most enterprising men to exert themselves to the best of their abilities in the service of all of the people.

6.

However, one does not exhaustively describe the sweeping changes that capitalism brought about in the conditions of the common man if one merely deals with the supremacy he enjoys on the market as a consumer and in the affairs of state as a voter and with the unprecedented improvement of his standard of living. No less important is the fact that capitalism has made it possible for him to save, to accumulate capital and to invest it. The gulf that in the pre-capitalistic status and caste society separated the owners of property from the penniless poor has been narrowed down. In older ages the journeyman had such a low pay that he could hardly lay by something and, if he nevertheless did so, he could only keep his savings by hoarding and hiding a few coins. Under capitalism his competence makes saving possible, and there are institutions that enable him to invest his funds in business. A not inconsiderable amount of the capital employed in American industries is the counterpart of the savings of employees. In acquiring savings deposits, insurance policies, bonds and also common stock, wage earners and salaried people are themselves earning interest and dividends and thereby, in the terminology of Marxism, are exploiters. The common man is directly interested in the flowering of business not only as a consumer and as an employee, but also as an investor. There prevails a tendency to efface to some extent the once sharp difference between those who own factors of production and those who do not. But, of course, this trend can only develop where the market economy is not sabotaged by allegedly social policies. The welfare state with its methods of easy money, credit expansion and undisguised inflation continually takes bites out of all claims payable in units of the nation's legal tender. The self-styled champions of the common man are still guided by the obsolete idea that a policy that favors the debtors at the expense of the creditors is very beneficial to the majority of the people. Their inability to comprehend the essential characteristics of the market economy manifests itself also in their failure to see the obvious fact that those whom they feign to aid are creditors in their capacity as savers, policy holders, and owners of bonds.

7.

The distinctive principle of Western social philosophy is individualism. It aims at the creation of a sphere in which the individual is free to think, to choose, and to act without being restrained by the interference of the social apparatus of coercion and oppression, the State. All the spiritual and material achievements of Western civilization were the result of the operation of this idea of liberty.

This doctrine and the policies of individualism and of capitalism, its application to economic matters, do not need any apologists or propagandists. The achievements speak for themselves.

The case for capitalism and private property rests, apart from other considerations, also upon the incomparable efficiency of its productive effort. It is this efficiency that makes it possible for capitalistic business to support a rapidly increasing population at a continually improving standard of living. The resulting progressive prosperity of the masses creates a social environment in which the exceptionally gifted individuals are free to give to their fellow-citizens all they are able to give. The social system of private property and limited government is the only system that tends to debarbarize all those who have the innate capacity to acquire personal culture.

It is a gratuitous pastime to belittle the material achievements of capitalism by observing that there are things that are more essential for mankind than bigger and speedier motorcars, and homes equipped with central heating, air conditioning, refrigerators, washing machines, and television sets. There certainly are such higher and nobler pursuits. But they are higher and nobler precisely because they cannot be aspired to by any external effort, but require the individual's personal determination and exertion. Those levelling this reproach against capitalism display a rather crude and materialistic view in assuming that moral and spiritual culture could be built either by the government or by the organization of production activities. All that these external factors can achieve in this regard is to bring about an environment and a competence which offers the individuals the opportunity to work at their own personal perfection and edification. It is not the fault of capitalism that the masses prefer a boxing match to a performance of Sophocles' Antigone, jazz music to Beethoven symphonies,and comics to poetry. But it is certain that while pre-capitalistic conditions as they still prevail in the much greater part of the world makes these good things accessible only to a small minority of people, capitalism gives to the many a favorable chance of striving after them.

From whatever angle one may look at capitalism there is no reason to lament the passing of the allegedly good old days. Still less is it justified to long for the totalitarian utopias, whether of the Nazi or of the Soviet type.

We are inaugurating tonight the ninth meeting of the Mont Pelerin Society. It is fitting to remember on this occasion that meetings of this kind in which opinions opposed to those of the majority of our contemporaries and to those of their governments are advanced and are possible only in the climate of liberty and freedom that is the most precious mark of Western civilization. Let us hope that this right to dissent will never disappear.

PLANNED CHAOS

This essay appeared in a 1947 monograph published by the Foundation for Economic Education and was later added as a postscript to the 1951 edition of *Socialism*.

Introductory Remarks

The characteristic mark of this age of dictators, wars and revolutions is its anti-capitalistic bias. Most governments and political parties are eager to restrict the sphere of private initiative and free enterprise. It is an almost unchallenged dogma that capitalism is done for and that the coming of all-round regimentation of economic activities is both inescapable and highly desirable.

None the less capitalism is still very vigorous in the Western Hemisphere. Capitalist production has made very remarkable progress even in these last years. Methods of production were greatly improved. Consumers have been supplied with better and cheaper goods and with many new articles unheard of a short time ago. Many countries have expanded the size and improved the quality of their manufacturing. In spite of the anti-capitalistic policies of all governments and of almost all political parties, the capitalist mode of production is in many countries still fulfilling its social function in supplying the consumers with more, better and cheaper goods.

It is certainly not a merit of governments, politicians and labour union officers that the standard of living is improving in the countries committed to the principle of private ownership of the means of production. Not offices and bureaucrats, but big business deserves credit for the fact that most of the families in the United States own a motor car and a radio set. The increase in per capita consumption in America as compared with conditions a quarter of a century ago is not an achievement of laws and executive orders. It is an accomplishment of business men who enlarged the size of their factories or built new ones.

One must stress this point because our contemporaries are inclined to ignore it. Entangled in the superstitions of statism and government omnipotence, they are exclusively preoccupied with governmental measures. They expect everything from authoritarian action and very little from the initiative of enterprising citizens. Yet, the only means to increase well-being is to increase the quantity of products. This is what business aims at.

It is grotesque that there is much more talk about the achievements of the Tennessee Valley Authority than about all the unprecedented and unparalleled achievements of American privately operated processing industries. However, it was only the latter which enabled the United Nations to win the war and today enables the United States to come to the aid of the Marshall Plan countries.

The dogma that the State or the Government is the embodiment of all that is good and beneficial and that the individuals are wretched underlings, exclusively intent upon inflicting harm upon one another and badly in need of a guardian, is almost unchallenged. It is taboo to question it in the slightest way. He who proclaims the godliness of the State and the infallibility of its priests, the bureaucrats, is considered as an impartial student of the social sciences. All those raising objections are branded as biased and narrow-minded. The supporters of the new religion of statolatry are no less fanatical and intolerant than were the Mohammedan conquerors of Africa and Spain.

History will call our age the age of the dictators and tyrants. We have witnessed in the last years the fall of two of these inflated supermen. But the spirit which raised these knaves to autocratic power survives. It permeates textbooks and periodicals, it speaks through the mouths of teachers and politicians, it manifests itself in party programmes and in plays and novels. As long as this spirit prevails there cannot be any hope of durable peace, of democracy, of the preservation of freedom or of a steady improvement in the nation's economic well-being.

1. The Failure of Interventionism

Nothing is more unpopular today than the free market economy, i.e., capitalism. Everything that is considered unsatisfactory in present-day conditions is charged to capitalism. The atheists make capitalism responsible for the survival of Christianity. But the papal encyclicals blame capitalism for the spread of irreligion and the sins of our contemporaries, and the Protestant churches and sects are no less vigorous in their indictment of capitalist greed. Friends of peace consider our wars as an offshoot of capitalist imperialism. But the adamant nationalist warmongers of Germany and Italy indicted capitalism for its "bourgeois" pacifism, contrary to human nature and to the inescapable laws of history. Sermonizers accuse capitalism of disrupting the family and fostering licentiousness. But the "progressives" blame capitalism for the preservation of allegedly outdated rules of sexual restraint. Almost all men agree that poverty is an outcome of capitalism. On the other hand many deplore the fact that capitalism, in catering lavishly to the wishes of people intent upon getting more amenities and a better living, promotes a crass materialism. These contradictory accusations of capitalism cancel one another.

But the fact remains that there are few people left who would not condemn capitalism altogether.

Although capitalism is the economic system of modern Western civilization, the policies of all Western nations are guided by utterly anti-capitalistic ideas. The aim of these interventionist policies is not to preserve capitalism, but to substitute a mixed economy for it. It is assumed that this mixed economy is neither capitalism nor socialism. It is described as a third system, as far from capitalism as it is from socialism. It is alleged that it stands midway between socialism and capitalism, retaining the advantages of both and avoiding the disadvantages inherent in each.

More than half a century ago the outstanding man in the British socialist movement, Sidney Webb, declared that the socialist philosophy is "but the conscious and explicit assertion of principles of social organization which have been already in great part unconsciously adopted." And he added that the economic history of the nineteenth century was "an almost continuous record of the progress of socialism."[10] A few years later an eminent British statesman, Sir William Harcourt, stated: "We are all socialists now."[11] When in 1913 an American, Elmer Roberts, published a book on the economic policies of the Imperial Government of Germany as conducted since the end of the 1870s, he called them "monarchical socialism."[12]

---

10 Sidney Webb, *Fabian Essays in Socialism*, first published in 1889 (American edition, New York, 1891, p. 4).

11 Cf. G. M. Trevelyan, *A Shortened History of England* (London, 1942), p. 510.

12 Elmer Roberts, *Monarchical Socialism in Germany* (New York, 1913).

However, it was not correct simply to identify interventionism and socialism. There are many supporters of interventionism who consider it the most appropriate method of realizing—step by step—full socialism. But there are also many interventionists who are not outright socialists; they aim at the establishment of the mixed economy as a permanent system of economic management. They endeavour to restrain, to regulate and to "improve" capitalism by government interference with business and by labour unionism.

In order to comprehend the working of interventionism and of the mixed economy it is necessary to clarify two points:

First: If within a society based on private ownership of the means of production some of these means are owned and operated by the government or by municipalities, this still does not make for a mixed system which would combine socialism and private ownership. As long as only certain individual enterprises are publicly controlled, the characteristics of the market economy determining economic activity remain essentially unimpaired. The publicly owned enterprises, too, as buyers of raw materials, semi-finished goods and labour, and as sellers of goods and services, must fit into the mechanism of the market economy. They are subject to the law of the market; they have to strive after profits or, at least, to avoid losses. When it is attempted to mitigate or to eliminate this dependence by covering the losses of such enterprises with subsidies out of public funds, the only result is a shifting of this dependence somewhere else. This is because the means for the subsidies have to be raised somewhere. They may be raised by collecting taxes. But the burden of such taxes has its effects on the public, not on the government collecting the tax. It is the market, and not the revenue department, which decides upon whom the burden of the tax falls and how it affects production and consumption. The market and its inescapable law are supreme.

Second: There are two different patterns for the realization of socialism. The one pattern—we may call it the Marxian or Russian pattern—is purely bureaucratic. All economic enterprises are departments of the government just as the administration of the army and the navy or the postal system. Every single plant, shop or farm, stands in the same relation to the superior central organization as does a post office to the office of the Postmaster-General. The whole nation forms one single labour army with compulsory service; the commander of this army is the chief of state.

The second pattern—we may call it the German or Zwangswirtschaft system[13] —differs from the first one in that it, seemingly and nominally, maintains private ownership of the means of production, entrepreneurship, and market exchange. So-called entrepreneurs do the buying and selling, pay the workers, contract debts and pay interest and amortization. But they are no longer entrepreneurs. In Nazi Germany they were called shop managers or Betriebsführer. The government tells these seeming entrepreneurs what and how to produce, at what prices and from whom to buy, at what prices and to whom to sell. The government decrees at what wages labourers should

13 *Zwang* means compulsion, *Wirtschaft* means economy. The English language equivalent for *Zwangswirtschaft* is something like compulsory economy.

work, and to whom and under what terms the capitalists should entrust their funds. Market exchange is but a sham. As all prices, wages and interest rates are fixed by the authority, they are prices, wages and interest rates in appearance only; in fact they are merely quantitative terms in the authoritarian orders determining each citizen's income, consumption and standard of living. The authority, not the consumers, directs production. The central board of production management is supreme; all citizens are nothing else but civil servants. This is socialism with the outward appearance of capitalism. Some labels of the capitalistic market economy are retained, but they signify here something entirely different from what they mean in the market economy.

It is necessary to point out this fact to prevent a confusion of socialism and interventionism. The system of the hampered market economy, or interventionism, differs from socialism by the very fact that it is still a market economy. The authority seeks to influence the market by the intervention of its coercive power, but it does not want to eliminate the market altogether. It desires that production and consumption should develop along lines different from those prescribed by the unhindered market, and it wants to achieve its aim by injecting into the working of the market orders, commands and prohibitions for whose enforcement the police power and its apparatus of coercion and compulsion stand ready. But these are isolated interventions; their authors assert that they do not plan to combine these measures into a completely integrated system which regulates all prices, wages and interest rates, and which thus places full control of production and consumption in the hands of the authorities.

However, all the methods of interventionism are doomed to

failure. This means: the interventionist measures must need result in conditions which from the point of view of their own advocates are more unsatisfactory than the previous state of affairs they were designed to alter. These policies are therefore contrary to purpose.

Minimum wage rates, whether enforced by government decree or by labour union pressure and compulsion, are useless if they fix wage rates at the market level. But if they try to raise wage rates above the level which the unhampered labour market would have determined, they result in permanent unemployment of a great part of the potential labour force.

Government spending cannot create additional jobs. If the government provides the funds required by taxing the citizens or by borrowing from the public, it abolishes on the one hand as many jobs as it creates on the other. If government spending is financed by borrowing from the commercial banks, it means credit expansion and inflation. If in the course of such an inflation the rise in commodity prices exceeds the rise in nominal wage rates, unemployment will drop. But what makes unemployment shrink is precisely the fact that real wage rates are falling.

The inherent tendency of capitalist evolution is to raise real wage rates steadily. This is the effect of the progressive accumulation of capital by means of which technological methods of production are improved. There is no means by which the height of wage rates can be raised for all those eager to earn wages other than through the increase of the per capita quota of capital invested. Whenever the accumulation of additional capital stops, the tendency towards a further increase in real wage rates comes to a standstill. If capital consumption is substituted for an increase in capital available, real wage rates must drop temporarily until the checks on a further increase in capital are removed. Government measures which retard capital accumulation or lead to capital consumption—such as confiscatory taxation—are therefore detrimental to the vital interests of the workers.

Credit expansion can bring about a temporary boom. But such a fictitious prosperity must end in a general depression of trade, a slump.

It can hardly be asserted that the economic history of the last decades has run counter to the pessimistic predictions of the economists. Our age has to face great economic troubles. But this is not a crisis of capitalism. It is the crisis of interventionism, of policies designed to improve capitalism and to substitute a better system for it.

No economist ever dared to assert that interventionism could result in anything else than in disaster and chaos. The advocates of interventionism--foremost among them the Prussian Historical School and the American Institutionalists—were not economists. On the contrary. In order to promote their plans they flatly denied that there is any such thing as economic law. In their opinion governments are free to achieve all they aim at without being restrained by an inexorable regularity in the sequence of economic phenomena Like the German socialist Ferdinand Lassalle, they maintain that the State is God.

The interventionists do not approach the study of economic matters with scientific disinterestedness. Most of them are driven by an envious resentment against those whose incomes are larger than their own. This bias makes it impossible for them to see things as they really are. For them the main thing is not to improve the conditions of the masses, but to harm the entrepreneurs and capitalists even if this policy victimizes the immense majority of the people.

In the eyes of the interventionists the mere existence of profits is objectionable. They speak of profit without dealing with its corollary, loss. They do not comprehend that profit and loss are the instruments by means of which the consumers keep a tight rein on all entrepreneurial activities. It is profit and loss that make the consumers supreme in the direction of business.It is absurd to contrast production for profit and production for use. On the unhampered market a man can earn profits only by supplying the consumers in the best and cheapest way with the goods they want to use. Profit and loss withdraw the material factors of production from the hands of the inefficient and place them in the hands of the more efficient. It is their social function to make a man the more influential in the conduct of business the better he succeeds in producing commodities for which people scramble. The consumers suffer when the laws of the country prevent the most efficient entrepreneurs from expanding the sphere of their activities. What made some enterprises develop into "big business" was precisely their success in filling best the demand of the masses.

Anti-capitalistic policies sabotage the operation of the capitalist system of the market economy. The failure of interventionism does not demonstrate the necessity of adopting socialism. It merely exposes the futility of interventionism. All those evils which the self-styled "progressives" interpret as evidence of the failure of capitalism are the outcome of their allegedly beneficial interference with the market. Only the ignorant, wrongly identifying interventionism and capitalism, believe that the remedy for these evils is socialism.

2. The Dictatorial, Anti-Democratic and Socialist Character of Interventionism

Many advocates of interventionism are bewildered when one tells them that in recommending interventionism they themselves are fostering anti-democratic and dictatorial tendencies and the establishment of totalitarian socialism. They protest that they are sincere believers and opposed to tyranny and socialism. What they aim at is only the improvement of the conditions of the poor. They say that they are driven by considerations of social justice, and favour a fairer distribution of income precisely because they are intent upon preserving capitalism and its political corollary or superstructure, viz., democratic government.

What these people fail to realize is that the various measures they suggest are not capable of bringing about the beneficial results aimed at. On the contrary they produce a state of affairs which from the point of view of their advocates is worse than the previous state which they were designed to alter. If the government, faced with this failure of its first intervention, is not prepared to undo its interference with the market and to return to a free economy, it must add to its first measure more and more regulations and restrictions. Proceeding step by step on this way it finally reaches a point in which all economic freedom of individuals has disappeared. Then socialism of the German pattern, the Zwangswirtschaft of the Nazis, emerges.

We have already mentioned the case of minimum wage rates. Let us illustrate the matter further by an analysis of a typical case of price control.

If the government wants to make it possible for poor parents to give more milk to their children, it must buy milk at the market price and sell it to those poor people with a loss at a cheaper rate; the loss may be covered from the means collected by taxation. But if the government simply fixes the price of milk at a lower rate than the market, the results obtained will be contrary to the aims of the government. The marginal producers will, in order to avoid losses, go out of the business of producing and selling milk. There will be less milk available for the consumers, not more. This outcome is contrary to the government's intentions. The government interfered because it considered milk as a vital necessity. It did not want to restrict its supply.

Now the government has to face the alternative: either to refrain from any endeavours to control prices, or to add to its first measure a second one, i.e., to fix the prices of the factors of production necessary for the production of milk. Then the same story repeats itself on a remoter plane: the government has again to fix the prices of the factors of production necessary for the production of those factors of production which are needed for the production of milk. Thus the government has to go further and further, fixing the prices of all the factors of production—both human (labour) and material—and forcing every entrepreneur and every worker to continue work at these prices and wages. No branch of production can be omitted from this all-round fixing of prices and wages and this general order to continue production. If some branches of production were left free, the result would be a shifting of capital and labour to them and a corresponding fall of the supply of the goods whose prices the government had fixed. However, it is precisely these goods which the government considers as especially important for the satisfaction of the needs of the masses.

But when this state of all-round control of business is achieved, the market economy has been replaced by a system of planned economy, by socialism. Of course, this is not the socialism of immediate state management of every plant by the government as in Russia, but the socialism of the German or Nazi pattern.

Many people were fascinated by the alleged success of German price control. They said: You have only to be as brutal and ruthless as the Nazis and you will succeed in controlling prices. What these people, eager to fight Nazism by adopting its methods, did not see was that the Nazis did not enforce price control within a market society, but they established a full socialist system, a totalitarian commonwealth.

Price control is contrary to purpose if it is limited to some commodities only. It cannot work satisfactorily within a market economy. If the government does not draw from this failure the conclusion that it must abandon all attempts to control prices, it must go further and further until it substitutes socialist all-round planning for the market economy.

Production can either be directed by the prices fixed on the market by the buying and by the abstention from buying on the part of the public. Or it can be directed by the government's central board of production management. There is no third solution available. There is no third social system feasible which would be neither market economy nor socialism. Government control of only a part of prices must result in a state of affairs which—without any exception—everybody considers as absurd and contrary to purpose. Its inevitable result is chaos and social unrest.

It is this that the economists have in mind in referring to economic law and asserting that interventionism is contrary to economic law.

In the market economy the consumers are supreme. Their buying and their abstention from buying ultimately determine what the entrepreneurs produce and in what quantity and quality. It determines directly the prices of the consumers' goods and indirectly the prices of all producers' goods, viz., labour and material factors of production. It determines the emergence of profits and losses and the formation of the rate of interest. It determines every individual's income. The focal point of the market economy is the market, i.e., the process of the formation of commodity prices, wage rates and interest rates and their derivatives, profits and losses. It makes all men in their capacity as producers responsible to the consumers. This dependence is direct with entrepreneurs, capitalists, farmers and professional men, and indirect with people working for salaries and wages. The market adjusts the efforts of all those engaged in supplying the needs of the consumers to the wishes of those for whom they produce, the consumers. It subjects production to consumption.

The market is a democracy in which every penny gives a right to vote. It is true that the various individuals have not the same power to vote. The richer man casts more ballots than the poorer fellow. But to be rich and to earn a higher income is, in the market economy, already the outcome of a previous election. The only means to acquire wealth and to preserve it, in a market economy not adulterated by government-made privileges and restrictions, is to serve the consumers in the best and cheapest way. Capitalists and landowners who fail in this regard suffer losses. If they do not change their procedure, they lose their wealth and become poor. It is consumers who make poor people rich and rich people poor. It is the consumers who fix the wages of a movie star and an opera singer at a higher level than those of a welder or an accountant.

Every individual is free to disagree with the outcome of an election campaign or of the market process. But in a democracy he has no other means to alter things than persuasion. If a man were to say: "I do not like the mayor elected by majority vote; therefore I ask the government to replace him by the man I prefer," one would hardly call him a democrat. But if the same claims are raised with regard to the market, most people are too dull to discover the dictatorial aspirations involved.

The consumers have made their choices and determined the income of the shoe manufacturer, the movie star and the welder. Who is Professor X to arrogate to himself the privilege of overthrowing their decision? If he were not a potential dictator, he would not ask the government to interfere. He would try to persuade his fellow citizens to increase their demand for the products of the welders and to reduce their demand for shoes and pictures.

The consumers are not prepared to pay for cotton prices which would render the marginal farms, i.e., those producing under the least favourable conditions, profitable. This is very unfortunate indeed for the farmers concerned; they must discontinue growing cotton and try to integrate themselves in another way into the whole of production.

But what shall we think of the statesman who interferes by

compulsion in order to raise the price of cotton above the level it would reach on the free market? What the interventionist aims at is the substitution of police pressure for the choice of the consumers. All this talk: the state should do this or that, ultimately means: the police should force consumers to behave otherwise than they would behave spontaneously. In such proposals as: let us raise farm prices, let us raise wage rates, let us lower profits, let us curtail the salaries of executives, the us ultimately refers to the police. Yet the authors of these projects protest that they are planning for freedom and industrial democracy.

In most non-socialist countries the labour unions are granted special rights. They are permitted to prevent non-members from working. They are allowed to call a strike and, when on strike, are virtually free to employ violence against all those who are prepared to continue working, viz., the strike-breakers. This system assigns an unlimited privilege to those engaged in vital branches of industry. Those workers whose strike cuts off the supply of water, light, food and other necessities are in a position to obtain all they want at the expense of the rest of the population. It is true that in the United States their unions have up to now exercised some moderation in taking advantage of this opportunity. Other American unions and many European unions have been less cautious. They are intent upon enforcing wage increases without bothering about the disaster inevitably resulting.

The interventionists are not shrewd enough to realize that labour union pressure and compulsion are absolutely incompatible with any system of social organization. The union problem has no reference whatsoever to the right of citizens to associate with one another in assemblies and associations; no democratic country denies its citizens this right. Neither does anybody dispute a man's right to stop work and to go on strike. The only question is whether or not the unions should be granted the privilege of resorting with impunity to violence. This privilege is no less incompatible with socialism than with capitalism. No social cooperation under the division of labour is possible when some people or unions of people are granted the right to prevent by violence and the threat of violence other people from working. When enforced by violence, a strike in vital branches of production or a general strike are tantamount to a revolutionary destruction of society.

A government abdicates if it tolerates any non-governmental agency's use of violence. If the government forsakes its monopoly of coercion and compulsion, anarchic conditions result. If it were true that a democratic system of government is unfit to protect unconditionally every individual's right to work in defiance of the orders of a union, democracy would be doomed. Then dictatorship would be the only means to preserve the division of labour and to avoid anarchy. What generated dictatorship in Russia and Germany was precisely the fact that the mentality of these nations made suppression of union violence unfeasible under democratic conditions. The dictators abolished strikes and thus broke the spine of labour unionism. There is no question of strikes in the Soviet empire.

It is illusory to believe that arbitration of labour disputes could bring the unions into the framework of the market economy and make their functioning compatible with the preservation of domestic peace. Judicial settlement of controversies is feasible if there is a set of rules available, according to which individual cases can be judged. But if such a code is valid and its provisions are applied to the determination of the height of wage rates, it is no longer the market which fixes them, but the code and those who legislate with regard to it. Then the government is supreme and no longer the consumers buying and selling on the market. If no such code exists, a standard according to which a controversy between employers and employees could be decided is lacking. It is vain to speak of "fair" wages in the absence of such a code. The notion of fairness is nonsensical if not related to an established standard. In practice, if the employers do not yield to the threats of the unions, arbitration is tantamount to the determination of wage rates by the government-appointed arbitrator. Peremptory authoritarian decision is substituted for the market price. The issue is always the same: the government or the market. There is no third solution.

Metaphors are often very useful in elucidating complicated problems and in making them comprehensible to less intelligent minds. But they become misleading and result in nonsense if people forget that every comparison is imperfect. It is silly to take metaphorical idioms literally and to deduce from their interpretation features of the object one wished to make more easily understandable by their use. There is no harm in the economists' description of the operation of the market as automatic and in their custom of speaking of the anonymous forces operating on the market. They could not anticipate that anybody would be so stupid as to take these metaphors literally.

No "automatic" and "anonymous" forces actuate the "mechanism" of the market. The only factors directing the market and determining prices are purposive acts of men. There is no automatism; there are men consciously aiming at ends chosen and deliberately resorting to definite means for the attainment of these ends. There are no mysterious mechanical forces; there is only the will of every individual to satisfy his demand for various goods. There is no anonymity; there are you and I and Bill and Joe and all the rest. And each of us is engaged both in production and consumption. Each contributes his share to the determination of prices.

The dilemma is not between automatic forces and planned action. It is between the democratic process of the market, in which every individual has his share, and the exclusive rule of a dictatorial body. Whatever people do in the market economy, is the execution of their own plans. In this sense every human action means planning. What those calling themselves planners advocate is not the substitution of planned action for letting things go. It is the substitution of the planner's own plan for the plans of his fellow men. The planner is a potential dictator who wants to deprive all other people of the power to plan and act according to their own plans. He aims at one thing only: the exclusive absolute pre-eminence of his own plan.

It is no less erroneous to declare that a government that is not socialistic has no plan. Whatever a government does is the execution of a plan, i.e., of a design. One may disagree with such a plan. But one must not say that it is not a plan at all. Professor Wesley C. Mitchell maintained that the British liberal government "planned to have no plan."[14] However, the British government in

---

14 Wesley C. Mitchell, "The Social Sciences and National Planning" in *Planned Society*, ed. Findlay Mackenzie (New York, 1937), p. 112

the liberal age certainly had a definite plan. Its plan was private ownership of the means of production, free initiative and a market economy. Great Britain was very prosperous indeed under this plan which according to Professor Mitchell is "no plan."

The planners pretend that their plans are scientific and that there cannot be disagreement with regard to them among well-intentioned and decent people. However, there is no such thing as a scientific ought. Science is competent to establish what is. It can never dictate what ought to be and what ends people should aim at. It is a fact that men disagree in their value judgments. It is insolent to arrogate to oneself the right to overrule the plans of other people and to force them to submit to the plan of the planner. Whose plan should be executed? The plan of the CIO or those of any other group? The plan of Trotsky or that of Stalin? The plan of Hitler or that of Strasser?

When people were committed to the idea that in the field of religion only one plan must be adopted, bloody wars resulted. With the acknowledgment of the principle of religious freedom these wars ceased. The market economy safeguards peaceful economic co-operation because it does not use force upon the economic plans of the citizens. If one master plan is to be substituted for the plans of each citizen, endless fighting must emerge. Those who disagree with the dictator's plan have no other means to carry on than to defeat the despot by force of arms.

It is an illusion to believe that a system of planned socialism could be operated according to democratic methods of government. Democracy is inextricably linked with capitalism. It cannot exist where there is planning. Let us refer to the words of the most eminent of the contemporary advocates of socialism.

Professor Harold Laski declared that the attainment of power by the British Labour Party in the normal parliamentary fashion must result in a radical transformation of parliamentary government. A socialist administration needs "guarantees" that its work of transformation would not be "disrupted" by repeal in event of its defeat at the polls. Therefore the suspension of the Constitution is "inevitable." [15] How pleased would Charles I and George III have been if they had known the books of Professor Laski!

Sidney and Beatrice Webb (Lord and Lady Passfield) tell us that "in any corporate action a loyal unity of thought is so important that, if anything is to be achieved, public discussion must be suspended between the promulgation of the decision and the accomplishment of the task." Whilst "the work is in progress" any expression of doubt, or even of fear that the plan will not be successful, is "an act of disloyalty, or even of treachery."[16] Now as the process of production never ceases and some work is always in progress and there is always something to be achieved, it follows that a socialist government must never concede any freedom of speech and the press. "A loyal unity of thought," what a high-sounding circumlocution for the ideals of Philip II and the Inquisition! In this regard another eminent admirer of the Soviets, Mr. T. G. Crowther, speaks without any reserve. He plainly declares that inquisition is "beneficial to science when it

---

15 Harold J. Laski, *Democracy in Crisis* (Chapel Hill, 1933), pp. 87-8.

16 Sidney and Beatrice Webb, *Soviet Communism: A New Civilization?* (New York, 1936), Vol. II, pp. 1038-39.

protects a rising class,"[17] i.e., when Mr. Crowther's friends resort to it. Hundreds of similar dicta could be quoted.

In the Victorian age, when John Stuart Mill wrote his essay On Liberty, such views as those held by Professor Laski, Mr. and Mrs. Webb and Mr. Crowther were called reactionary. Today they are called "progressive" and "liberal." On the other hand people who oppose the suspension of parliamentary government and of the freedom of speech and the press and the establishment of inquisition are scorned as "reactionaries," as "economic royalists" and as "Fascists."

Those interventionists who consider interventionism as a method of bringing about full socialism step by step are at least consistent. If the measures adopted fail to achieve the beneficial results expected and end in disaster, they ask for more and more government interference until the government has taken over the direction of all economic activities. But those interventionists who look at interventionism as a means of improving capitalism and thereby preserving it are utterly confused.

In the eyes of these people all the undesired and undesirable effects of government interference with business are caused by capitalism. The very fact that a governmental measure has brought about a state of affairs which they dislike is for them a justification of further measures. They fail, for instance, to realize that the role monopolistic schemes play in our time is the effect of government interference such as tariffs and patents. They advocate government action for the prevention of monopoly. One

---

17 T. G. Crowther, *Social Relations of Science* (London, 1941), p. 333.

could hardly imagine a more unrealistic idea. For the governments whom they ask to fight monopoly are the same governments who are devoted to the principle of monopoly. Thus, the American New Deal Government embarked upon a thorough-going monopolistic organization of every branch of American business, by the NRA, and aimed at organizing American farming as a vast monopolistic scheme, restricting farm output for the sake of substituting monopoly prices for the lower market prices. It was a party to various international commodity control agreements the undisguised aim of which was to establish international monopolies of various commodities. The same is true of all other governments. The Union of Soviet Socialist Republics was also a party to some of these intergovernmental monopolistic conventions.[18] Its repugnance for collaboration with the capitalistic countries was not so great as to cause it to miss any opportunity for fostering monopoly.

The programme of this self-contradictory interventionism is dictatorship, supposedly to make people free. But the liberty its supporters advocate is liberty to do the "right" things, i.e., the things they themselves want to be done. They are not only ignorant of the economic problem involved. They lack the faculty of logical thinking.

The most absurd justification of interventionism is provided by those who look upon the conflict between capitalism and socialism as if it were a contest over the distribution of income.

---

18 The collection of these conventions, published by The International Labour Office under the title Intergovernmental Commodity Control Agreements (Montreal, 1943).

Why should not the propertied classes be more compliant? Why should they not accord to the poor workers a part of their ample revenues? Why should they oppose the government's design to raise the share of the underprivileged by decreeing minimum wage rates and maximum prices and by cutting profits and interest rates down to a "fairer" level? Pliability in such matters, they say, would take the wind from the sails of the radical revolutionaries and preserve capitalism. The worst enemies of capitalism, they say, are those intransigent doctrinaires whose excessive advocacy of economic freedom, of laissez-faire and Manchesterism renders vain all attempts to come to a compromise with the claims of labour. These adamant reactionaries are alone responsible for the bitterness of contemporary party strife and the implacable hatred it generates. What is needed is the substitution of a constructive programme for the purely negative attitude of the economic royalists. And, of course, "constructive" is in the eyes of these people only interventionism.

However, this mode of reasoning is entirely vicious. It takes for granted that the various measures of government interference with business will attain those beneficial results which their advocates expect from them. It blithely disregards all that economics says about their futility in attaining the ends sought, and their unavoidable and undesirable consequences. The question is not whether minimum wage rates are fair or unfair, but whether or not they bring about unemployment of a part of those eager to work. By calling these measures just, the interventionist does not refute the objections raised against their expediency by the economists. He merely displays ignorance of the question at issue.

The conflict between capitalism and socialism is not a contest between two groups of claimants concerning the size of the portions to be allotted to each of them out of a definite supply of goods. It is a dispute concerning what system of social organization best serves human welfare. Those fighting socialism do not reject socialism because they envy the workers the benefits they (the workers) could allegedly derive from the socialist mode of production. They fight socialism precisely because they are convinced that it would harm the masses in reducing them to the status of poor serfs entirely at the mercy of irresponsible dictators.

In this conflict of opinions everybody must make up his mind and take a definite stand. Everybody must side either with the advocates of economic freedom or with those of totalitarian socialism. One cannot evade this dilemma by adopting an allegedly middle-of-the-road position, namely interventionism. For interventionism is neither a middle way nor a compromise between capitalism and socialism. It is a third system. It is a system the absurdity and futility of which is agreed upon not only by all economists but even by the Marxians.

There is no such thing as an "excessive" advocacy of economic freedom. On the one hand, production can be directed by the efforts of each individual to adjust his conduct so as to fill the most urgent wants of the consumers in the most appropriate way. This is the market economy. On the other hand, production can be directed by authoritarian decree. If these decrees concern only some isolated items of the economic structure, they fail to attain the ends sought, and their own advocates do not like their outcome. If they come up to all-round regimentation, they mean totalitarian socialism.

Men must choose between the market economy and socialism.

The state can preserve the market economy in protecting life, health and private property against violent or fraudulent aggression; or it can itself control the conduct of all production activities. Some agency must determine what should be produced. If it is not the consumers by means of demand and supply on the market, it must be the government by compulsion.

3. Socialism and Communism

In the terminology of Marx and Engels the words communism and socialism are synonymous. They are alternately applied without any distinction between them. The same was true for the practice of all Marxian groups and sects until 1917. The political parties of Marxism which considered the Communist Manifesto as the unalterable gospel of their doctrine called themselves socialist parties. The most influential and most numerous of these parties, the German party, adopted the name Social Democratic Party. In Italy, in France and in all other countries in which Marxian parties already played a role in political life before 1917, the term socialist likewise superseded the term communist. No Marxian ever ventured, before 1917, to distinguish between communism and socialism.

In 1875, in his Criticism of the Gotha Programme of the German Social Democratic Party, Marx distinguished between a lower (earlier) and a higher (later) phase of the future communist society. But he did not reserve the name of communism to the higher phase, and did not call the lower phase socialism as differentiated from communism.

One of the fundamental dogmas of Marx is that socialism is bound to come "with the inexorability of a law of nature." Capitalist production begets its own negation and establishes the socialist system of public ownership of the means of production. This process "executes itself through the operation of the inherent laws of capitalist production."[19] It is independent of the wills of people.[20] It is impossible for men to accelerate it, to delay it or to hinder it. For "no social system ever disappears before all the productive forces are developed for the development of which it is broad enough, and new higher methods of production never appear before the material conditions of their existence have been hatched out in the womb of previous society."[21]

This doctrine is, of course, irreconcilable with Marx's own political activities and with the teachings he advanced for the justification of these activities. Marx tried to organize a political party which by means of revolution and civil war should accomplish the transition from capitalism to socialism. The characteristic feature of their parties was, in the eyes of Marx and all Marxian doctrinaires, that they were revolutionary parties invariably committed to the idea of violent action. Their aim was to rise in rebellion, to establish the dictatorship of the proletarians and to exterminate

---

19 Karl Marx, *Das Kapital*, 7th ed. (Hamburg, 1914), Vol. I, p. 728. Publisher's Note: In English edition, p. 836.

20 Karl Marx, *Zur Kritik der politischen Ökonomie*, ed. Kautsky (Stuttgart, 1897), p. xi. Publisher's Note: In English edition by Kerr, pp. 11-12; by Eastman, p. 10.

21 Ibid., p. xii. Publisher's Note: In English edition by Kerr, p. 12; by Eastman, p. 11.

mercilessly all bourgeois. The deeds of the Paris Communards in 1871 were considered as the perfect model of such a civil war. The Paris revolt, of course, had lamentably failed. But later uprisings were expected to succeed. [22]

However, the tactics applied by the Marxian parties in various European countries were irreconcilably opposed to each of these two contradictory varieties of the teachings of Karl Marx. They did not place confidence in the inevitability of the coming of socialism. Neither did they trust in the success of a revolutionary upheaval. They adopted the methods of parliamentary action. They solicited votes in election campaigns and sent their delegates into the parliaments. They "degenerated" into democratic parties. In the parliaments they behaved like other parties of the opposition. In some countries they entered into temporary alliances with other parties, and occasionally socialist members sat in the cabinets. Later, after the end of the first World War, the socialist parties became paramount in many parliaments. In some countries they ruled exclusively, in others in close cooperation with "bourgeois" parties.

It is true that these domesticated socialists before 1917 never abandoned lip service to the rigid principles of orthodox Marxism. They repeated again and again that the coming of socialism is unavoidable. They emphasized the inherent revolutionary character of their parties. Nothing could arouse their anger more than when somebody dared to dispute their adamant revolutionary spirit.

22 Karl Marx, *Der Bürgerkrieg in Frankreich*, ed. Pfemfert (Berlin, 1919), passim. Publisher's Note: In English, "The Civil War in France." Reprinted in Eastman anthology, pp. 367-429.

However, in fact they were parliamentary parties like all other parties.

From a correct Marxian point of view, as expressed in the later writings of Marx and Engels (but not yet in the Communist Manifesto), all measures designed to restrain, to regulate and to improve capitalism were simply "petty-bourgeois" nonsense stemming from an ignorance of the immanent laws of capitalist evolution. True socialists should not place any obstacles in the way of capitalist evolution. For only the full maturity of capitalism could bring about socialism. It is not only vain, but harmful to the interests of the proletarians to resort to such measures. Even labour-unionism is not an adequate means for the improvement of the conditions of the workers.[23] Marx did not believe that interventionism could benefit the masses. He violently rejected the idea that such measures as minimum wage rates, price ceilings, restriction of interest rates, social security and so on are preliminary steps in bringing about socialism. He aimed at the radical abolition of the wages system which can be accomplished only by communism in its higher phase. He would have sarcastically ridiculed the idea of abolishing the "commodity character" of labour within the frame of a capitalist society by the enactment of a law.

But the socialist parties as they operated in the European countries were virtually no less committed to interventionism than the Sozialpolitik of the Kaiser's Germany and the American New Deal. It was against this policy that George Sorel and Syndicalism directed their attacks. Sorel, a timid intellectual of a bourgeois

---

23 Karl Marx, *Value, Price and Profit*, ed. Eleanor Marx Aveling (New York, 1901), pp. 72-74.

background, deprecated the "degeneration" of the socialist parties for which he blamed their penetration by bourgeois intellectuals. He wanted to see the spirit of ruthless aggressiveness, inherent in the masses, revived and freed from the guardianship of intellectual cowards. For Sorel nothing counted but riots. He advocated action directe, i.e., sabotage and the general strike, as initiatory steps towards the final great revolution.

Sorel had success mostly among snobbish and idle intellectuals and no less snobbish and idle heirs of wealthy entrepreneurs. He did not perceptibly move the masses. For the Marxian parties in Western and Central Europe his passionate criticism was hardly more than a nuisance. His historical importance consisted mainly in the role his ideas played in the evolution of Russian Bolshevism and Italian Fascism.

In order to understand the mentality of the Bolshevists we must again refer to the dogmas of Karl Marx. Marx was fully convinced that capitalism is a stage of economic history which is not limited to a few advanced countries only. Capitalism has the tendency to convert all parts of the world into capitalist countries. The bourgeoisie forces all nations to become capitalist nations. When the final hour of capitalism sounds, the whole world will be uniformly in the stage of mature capitalism, ripe for the transition to socialism. Socialism will emerge at the same time in all parts of the world.

Marx erred on this point no less than in all his other statements. Today even the Marxians cannot and do not deny that there still prevail enormous differences in the development of capitalism in various countries. They realize that there are many countries which, from the point of view of the Marxian interpretation of history, must be described as precapitalistic. In these countries the bourgeoisie has not yet attained a ruling position and has not yet set the historical stage of capitalism which is the necessary prerequisite of the appearance of socialism. These countries therefore must first accomplish their "bourgeois revolution" and must go through all phases of capitalism before there can be any question of transforming them into socialist countries. The only policy which Marxians could adopt in such countries would be to support the bourgeois unconditionally, first in their endeavours to seize power and then in their capitalistic ventures. A Marxian party could for a very long time have no other task than to be subservient to bourgeois liberalism. This alone is the mission which historical materialism, if consistently applied, could assign to Russian Marxians. They would be forced to wait quietly until capitalism should have made their nation ripe for socialism.

But the Russian Marxians did not want to wait. They resorted to a new modification of Marxism according to which it was possible for a nation to skip one of the stages of historical evolution. They shut their eyes to the fact that this new doctrine was not a modification of Marxism, but rather the denial of the last remnant which was left of it. It was an undisguised return to the pre-Marxian and anti-Marxian socialist teachings according to which men are free to adopt socialism at any time if they consider it as a system more beneficial to the commonweal than capitalism. It utterly exploded all the mysticism inwrought into dialectical materialism and in the alleged Marxian discovery of the inexorable laws of mankind's economic evolution.

Having emancipated themselves from Marxian determinism, the Russian Marxians were free to discuss the most appropriate tactics for the realization of socialism in their country. They were no longer bothered with economic problems. They had no longer to investigate whether or not the time had come. They had only one task to accomplish, the seizure of the reins of government.

One group maintained that lasting success could be expected only if the support of a sufficient number of the people, though not necessarily of the majority, could be won. Another group did not favour such a time-consuming procedure. They suggested a bold stroke. A small group of fanatics should be organized as the vanguard of the revolution. Strict discipline and unconditional obedience to the chief should make these professional revolutionists fit for a sudden attack. They should supplant the Czarist government and then rule the country according to the traditional methods of the Czar's police.

The terms used to signify these two groups—Bolshevists (majority) for the latter and Mensheviks (minority) for the former—refer to a vote taken in 1903 at a meeting held for the discussion of these tactical issues. The only difference dividing the two groups from one another was this matter of tactical methods. They both agreed with regard to the ultimate end: socialism.

Both sects tried to justify their respective points of view by quoting passages from Marx's and Engels's writings. This is, of course, the Marxian custom. And each sect was in a position to discover in these sacred books dicta confirming its own stand.

Lenin, the Bolshevist chief, knew his countrymen much better than his adversaries and their leader, Plekhanov, did. He did not, like Plekhanov, make the mistake of applying to Russians the standards of the Western nations. He remembered how foreign women had twice simply usurped supreme power and quietly ruled for a lifetime. He was aware of the fact that the terrorist methods of the Czar's secret police were successful and he was confident that he could considerably improve on these methods. He was a ruthless dictator and he knew that the Russians lacked the courage to resist oppression. Like Cromwell, Robespierre and Napoleon, he was an ambitious usurper and fully trusted the absence of revolutionary spirit in the immense majority. The autocracy of the Romanovs was doomed because the unfortunate Nicholas II was a weakling. The socialist lawyer Kerensky failed because he was committed to the principle of parliamentary government. Lenin succeeded because he never aimed at anything else than his own dictatorship. And the Russians yearned for a dictator, for a successor of the Terrible Ivan.

The rule of Nicholas II was not ended by a real revolutionary upheaval. It collapsed on the battlefields. Anarchy resulted which Kerensky could not master. A skirmish in the streets of Saint Petersburg removed Kerensky. A short time later Lenin had his eighteenth Brumaire. In spite of all the terror practised by the Bolshevists the Constituent Assembly, elected by universal franchise for men and women, had only about twenty per cent Bolshevist members. Lenin dispelled by force of arms the Constituent Assembly. The short-lived "liberal" interlude was liquidated. Russia passed from the hands of the inept Romanovs into those of a real autocrat.

Lenin did not content himself with the conquest of Russia.

He was fully convinced that he was destined to bring the bliss of socialism to all nations, not only to Russia. The official name which he chose for his government—Union of the Soviet Socialist Republics —does not contain any reference to Russia. It was designed as the nucleus of a world government. It was implied that all foreign comrades by rights owed allegiance to this government and that all foreign bourgeois who dared to resist were guilty of high treason and deserved capital punishment. Lenin did not doubt in the least that all Western countries were on the eve of the great final revolution. He daily expected its outbreak.

There was in the opinion of Lenin only one group in Europe that might—although without any prospect of success—try to prevent the revolutionary upheaval: the depraved members of the intelligentsia who had usurped the leadership of the socialist parties. Lenin had long hated these men for their addiction to parliamentary procedure and their reluctance to endorse his dictatorial aspirations. He raged against them because he held them responsible for the fact that the socialist parties had supported the war effort of their countries. Already in his Swiss exile, which ended in 1917, Lenin began to split the European socialist parties. Now he set up a new, a Third International which he controlled in the same dictatorial manner in which he directed the Russian Bolshevists. For this new party Lenin chose the name Communist Party. The communists were to fight unto death the various European socialist parties, these "social traitors," and they were to arrange the immediate liquidation of the bourgeoisie and seizure of power by the armed workers. Lenin did not differentiate between socialism and communism as social systems. The goal which he aimed at was not called communism as opposed to socialism. The official name of the Soviet government is Union of the Socialist (not of the Communist) Soviet Republics. In this regard he did not want to alter the traditional terminology which considered the terms as synonymous. He merely called his partisans, the only sincere and consistent supporters of the revolutionary principles of orthodox Marxism, communists and their tactical methods communism because he wanted to distinguish them from the "treacherous hirelings of the capitalist exploiters," the wicked Social Democratic leaders like Kautsky and Albert Thomas. These traitors, he emphasized, were anxious to preserve capitalism. They were not true socialists. The only genuine Marxians were those who rejected the name of socialists, irremediably fallen into disrepute.

Thus the distinction between communists and socialists came into being. Those Marxians who did not surrender to the dictator in Moscow called themselves social democrats or, in short, socialists. What characterized them was the belief that the most appropriate method for the realization of their plans to establish socialism, the final goal common to them as well as to the communists, was to win the support of the majority of their fellow citizens. They abandoned the revolutionary slogans and tried to adopt democratic methods for the seizure of power. They did not bother about the problem whether or not a socialist regime is compatible with democracy. But for the attainment of socialism they were resolved to apply democratic procedures.

The communists, on the other hand, were in the early years of the Third International firmly committed to the principle of revolution and civil war. They were loyal only to their Russian chief. They expelled from their ranks everybody who was suspected of feeling himself bound by any of his country's laws. They plotted unceasingly and squandered blood in unsuccessful riots.

Lenin could not understand why the communists failed everywhere outside Russia. He did not expect much from the American workers. In the United States, the communists agreed, the workers lacked the revolutionary spirit because they were spoiled by well-being and steeped in the vice of money-making. But Lenin did not doubt that the European masses were class-conscious and therefore fully committed to revolutionary ideas. The only reason why the revolution had not been realized was in his opinion the inadequacy and cowardice of the communist officials. Again and again he deposed his vicars and appointed new men. But he did not succeed any better.

In the Anglo-Saxon and in the Latin-American countries the socialist voters place confidence in democratic methods. Here the number of people who seriously aim at a communist revolution is very small. Most of those who publicly proclaim their adherence to the principles of communism would feel extremely unhappy if the revolution were to arise and expose their lives and their property to danger. If the Russian armies were to march into their countries or if domestic communists were to seize power without engaging them in the fight, they would probably rejoice in the hope of being rewarded for their Marxian orthodoxy. But they themselves do not long for revolutionary laurels.

It is a fact that in all these thirty years of passionate pro-Soviet agitation not a single country outside Russia went communist of its citizens' own accord. Eastern Europe turned to communism only when the diplomatic arrangements of international power politics had converted it into a sphere of exclusive Russian influence and hegemony. It is unlikely that Western Germany, France, Italy and Spain will espouse communism if the United States and Great Britain do not adopt a policy of absolute diplomatic "désintéressement." What gives strength to the communist movement in these and in some other countries is the belief that Russia is driven by an unflinching "dynamism" while the Anglo-Saxon powers are indifferent and not very much interested in their fate.

Marx and the Marxians erred lamentably when they assumed that the masses long for a revolutionary overthrow of the "bourgeois" order of society. The militant communists are to be found only in the ranks of those who make a living from their communism or expect that a revolution would further their personal ambitions. The subversive activities of these professional plotters are dangerous precisely on account of the naivety of those who are merely flirting with the revolutionary idea. Those confused and misguided sympathizers who call themselves "liberals" and whom the communists call "useful innocents," the fellow travellers and even the majority of the officially registered party members, would be terribly frightened if they were to discover one day that their chiefs mean business when preaching sedition. But then it may be too late to avert disaster.

For the time being, the ominous peril of the communist parties in the West lies in their stand on foreign affairs. The distinctive mark of all present-day communist parties is their devotion to the aggressive foreign policy of the Soviets. Whenever they must choose between Russia and their own country, they do not hesitate to prefer Russia. Their principle is: Right or wrong, my Russia. They strictly obey all orders issued from Moscow. When

Russia was an ally of Hitler, the French communists sabotaged their own country's war effort and the American communists passionately opposed President Roosevelt's plans to aid England and France in their struggle against the Nazis. The communists all over the world branded all those who defended themselves against the German invaders as "imperialist warmongers." But as soon as Hitler attacked Russia, the imperialist war of the capitalists changed overnight into a just war of defence. Whenever Stalin conquers one more country, the communists justify this aggression as an act of self-defence against "Fascists."

In their blind worship of everything that is Russian, the communists of Western Europe and the United States by far surpass the worst excesses ever committed by chauvinists. They wax rapturous about Russian movies, Russian music and the alleged discoveries of Russian science. They speak in ecstatic words about the economic achievements of the Soviets. They ascribe the victory of the United Nations to the deeds of the Russian armed forces. Russia, they contend, has saved the world from the Fascist menace. Russia is the only free country while all other nations are subject to the dictatorship of the capitalists. The Russians alone are happy and enjoy the bliss of living a full life; in the capitalist countries the immense majority are suffering from frustration and unfulfilled desires. Just as the pious Muslim yearns for a pilgrimage to the Prophet's tomb at Mecca, so the communist intellectual deems a pilgrimage to the holy shrines of Moscow as the event of his life.

However, the distinction in the use of the terms communists and socialists did not affect the meaning of the terms communism and socialism as applied to the final goal of the policies common to them both. It was only in 1928 that the programme of the Communist International, adopted by the sixth congress in Moscow,[24] began to differentiate between communism and socialism (and not merely between communists and socialists).

According to this new doctrine there is, in the economic evolution of mankind, between the historical stage of capitalism and that of communism, a third stage, namely that of socialism. Socialism is a social system based on public control of the means of production and full management of all processes of production and distribution by a planning central authority. In this regard it is equal to communism. But it differs from communism in so far as there is no equality of the portions allotted to each individual for his own consumption. There are still wages paid to the comrades and these wage rates are graduated according to economic expediency as far as the central authority deems it necessary for securing the greatest possible output of products. What Stalin calls socialism corresponds by and large to Marx's concept of the "early phase" of communism. Stalin reserves the term communism exclusively for what Marx called the "higher phase" of communism. Socialism, in the sense in which Stalin has lately used the term, is moving towards communism, but is in itself not yet communism. Socialism will turn into communism as soon as the increase in wealth to be expected from the operation of the socialist methods of production has raised the lower standard of living of the Russian masses to the higher

---

24 *Blueprint for World Conquest as Outlined by the Communist International*, Human Events (Washington and Chicago, 1946), pp. 181-82.

standard which the distinguished holders of important offices enjoy in present-day Russia.[25]

The apologetical character of this new terminological practice is obvious. Stalin finds it necessary to explain to the vast majority of his subjects why their standard of living is extremely low, much lower than that of the masses in the capitalist countries and even lower than that of the Russian proletarians in the days of Czarist rule. He wants to justify the fact that salaries and wages are unequal, that a small group of Soviet officials enjoys all the luxuries modern technique can provide, that a second group, more numerous than the first one, but less numerous than the middle class in imperial Russia, lives in "bourgeois" style, while the masses, ragged and barefooted, subsist in congested slums and are poorly fed. He can no longer blame capitalism for this state of affairs. Thus he was compelled to resort to a new ideological makeshift.

Stalin's problem was the more burning as the Russian communists in the early days of their rule had passionately proclaimed income equality as a principle to be enforced from the first instant of the proletarians' seizure of power. Moreover, in the capitalist countries the most powerful demagogic trick applied by the Russia-sponsored communist parties is to excite the envy of those with lower incomes against all those with higher incomes. The main argument advanced by the communists for the support of their thesis that Hitler's National Socialism was not genuine socialism, but, on the contrary, the worst variety of

25 David J. Dallin, *The Real Soviet Russia* (Yale University Press, 1944), pp. 88-95.

capitalism, was that there was in Nazi Germany inequality in the standard of living.

Stalin's new distinction between socialism and communism is in open contradiction to the policy of Lenin, and no less to the tenets of the propaganda of the communist parties outside the Russian frontiers. But such contradictions do not matter in the realm of the Soviets. The word of the dictator is the ultimate decision, and nobody is so foolhardy as to venture opposition.

It is important to realize that Stalin's semantical innovation affects merely the terms communism and socialism. He did not alter the meaning of the terms socialist and communist. The Bolshevist party is just as before called communist. The Russophile parties beyond the borders of the Soviet Union call themselves communist parties and are violently fighting the socialist parties which, in their eyes, are simply social traitors. But the official name of the Union of Soviet Socialist Republics remains unchanged.

4. Russia's Aggressiveness

The German, Italian and Japanese nationalists justified their aggressive policies by their lack of *Lebensraum*. Their countries are comparatively over-populated. They are poorly endowed by nature and depend on the import of foodstuffs and raw materials from abroad. They must export manufactures to pay for these badly needed imports. But the protectionist policies espoused by the countries producing a surplus of foodstuffs and raw materials close their frontiers to import of manufactures. The world is manifestly tending towards a state of full economic autarky of each nation. In such a world, what fate is in store for those nations who can neither feed nor clothe their citizens out of domestic resources?

The *Lebensraum* doctrine of the self-styled "have-not" peoples emphasizes that there are in America and in Australia millions of acres of unused land much more fertile than the barren soil which the farmers of the have-not nations are tilling. Natural conditions for mining and manufacturing are likewise much more propitious than in the countries of the have-nots. But the German, Italian and Japanese peasants and workers are barred from access to these areas favoured by nature. The immigration laws of the comparatively underpopulated countries prevent their migration. These laws raise the marginal productivity of labour and thereby wage rates in the underpopulated countries and lower them in the overpopulated countries. The high standard of living in the United States and the British Dominions is paid for by a lowering of the standard of living in the congested countries of Europe and Asia.

The true aggressors, say these German, Italian and Japanese nationalists, are those nations who by means of trade and migration barriers have arrogated to themselves the lion's share of the natural riches of the earth. Has not the Pope[26] himself declared that the root causes of the World Wars are "that cold and calculating egoism which tends to hoard the economic resources and materials destined for the use of all to such an extent that the nations less favoured by nature are not permitted access to

26 Pius XII (pope, 1939-1958) (Pub.).

them"?[27] The war that Hitler, Mussolini and Hirohito kindled was from this point of view a just war, for its only aim was to give to the have-nots what, by virtue of natural and divine right, belongs to them.

The Russians cannot venture to justify their aggressive policy by such arguments. Russia is a comparatively underpopulated country. Its soil is much better endowed by nature than that of any other nation. It offers the most advantageous conditions for the growing of all kinds of cereals, fruits, seeds and plants. Russia owns immense pastures and almost inexhaustible forests. It has the richest resources for the production of gold, silver, platinum, iron, copper, nickel, manganese and all other metals, and of oil. But for the despotism of the Czars and the lamentable inadequacy of the communist system, its population could long since have enjoyed the highest standard of living. It is certainly not lack of natural resources that pushes Russia towards conquest.

Lenin's aggressiveness was an outgrowth of his conviction that he was the leader of the final world revolution. He considered himself as the legitimate successor of the First International, destined to accomplish the task in which Marx and Engels had failed. The knell of capitalism had sounded, and no capitalist machinations could delay the expropriation of the expropriators any longer. What was needed was only the dictator of the new social order. Lenin was ready to take the burden upon his shoulders.

Since the days of the Mongol invasions mankind has not had to face such an unflinching and thorough-going aspiration

---

27 Christmas Eve broadcast, New York Times, December 25, 1941.

for unlimited world supremacy. In every country the Russian emissaries and the communist fifth columns were fanatically working for the "Anschluss" to Russia. But Lenin lacked the first four columns. Russia's military forces were at that time contemptible. When they crossed the Russian borders, they were stopped by the Poles. They could not march further West. The great campaign for world conquest petered out.

It was just idle talk to discuss the problems whether communism in one country only is possible or desirable. The communists had failed utterly outside the Russian frontiers. They were forced to stay at home.

Stalin devoted all his energy to the organization of a standing army of a size the world had never seen before. But he was not more successful than Lenin and Trotsky had been. The Nazis easily defeated this army and occupied the most important part of Russia's territory. Russia was saved by the British and, above all, by the American forces. American Lend-Lease enabled the Russians to follow on the heels of the Germans when the scarcity of equipment and the threatening American invasion forced them to withdraw from Russia. They could even occasionally defeat the rearguards of the retreating Nazis. They could conquer Berlin and Vienna when the American airplanes had smashed the German defences. When the Americans had crushed the Japanese, the Russians could quietly stab them in the back.

Of course, the communists inside and outside of Russia and the fellow-travellers passionately contend that it was Russia that defeated the Nazis and liberated Europe. They pass over in silence the fact that the only reason why the Nazis could not capture Moscow, Leningrad and Stalingrad was their lack of munitions, airplanes and gasoline. It was the blockade that made it impossible for the Nazis to provide their armies with the equipment needed, and to construct in the occupied Russian territory a transport system that could ship this equipment to the far distant front line. The decisive battle of the war was the battle of the Atlantic. The great strategical events in the war against Germany were the conquest of Africa and Sicily and the victory in Normandy. Stalingrad was, when measured by the gigantic standards of this war, hardly more than a tactical success. In the struggle against the Italians and the Japanese, Russia's share was nil.

But the spoils of the victory go to Russia alone. While the other United Nations do not seek for territorial aggrandizement, the Russians are in full swing. They have annexed the three Baltic Republics, Bessarabia, Czechoslovakia's province of Carpatho-Russia,[28] a part of Finland, a great part of Poland and huge territories in the Far East. They claim the rest of Poland, Rumania, Hungary, Yugoslavia, Bulgaria, Korea and China as their exclusive sphere of influence. They are anxious to establish in these countries "friendly" governments, i.e. puppet governments. But for the opposition raised by the United States and Great Britain they would rule today in the whole of continental Europe, continental Asia and Northern Africa. Only the American and British garrisons in Germany bar the Russians' way to the shores of the Atlantic.

Today, no less than after the first World War, the real menace for the West does not lie in the military power of Russia. Great

28 The annexation of Carpatho-Russia utterly explodes their hypocritical indignation about the Munich agreements of 1938.

Britain could easily repel a Russian attack and it would be sheer lunacy for the Russians to undertake a war against the United States. Not the Russian armies, but the communist ideologies threaten the West. The Russians know it very well and place confidence not in their own army, but in their foreign partisans. They want to overthrow the democracies from within, not from without. Their main weapon is the pro-Russian machinations of their Fifth Columns. These are the crack divisions of Bolshevism.

The communist writers and politicians inside and outside of Russia explain Russia's aggressive policies as mere self-defence. It is, they say, not Russia that plans aggression but, on the contrary, the decaying capitalist democracies. Russia wants merely to defend its own independence. This is an old and well-tried method of justifying aggression. Louis XIV and Napoleon I, Wilhelm II and Hitler were the most peace-loving of all men. When they invaded foreign countries, they did so only in just self-defence. Russia was as much menaced by Estonia or Latvia as Germany was by Luxemburg or Denmark.

An outgrowth of this fable of self-defence is the legend of the cordon sanitaire. The political independence of the small neighbour countries of Russia, it is maintained, is merely a capitalist makeshift designed to prevent the European democracies from being infected with the germ of communism. Hence, it is concluded, these small nations have forfeited their right to independence. For Russia has the inalienable right to claim that its neighbours—and likewise its neighbours' neighbours—should only be ruled by "friendly," i.e., strictly communist, governments. What would happen to the world if all great powers were to make the same pretension?

The truth is that it is not the governments of the democratic nations that aim at overthrowing the present Russian system. They do not foster pro-democratic fifth columns in Russia and they do not incite the Russian masses against their rulers. But the Russians are busy day and night fomenting unrest in every country.

The very lame and hesitant intervention of the Allied Nations in the Russian Civil War was not a pro-capitalist and anti-communist venture. For the Allied Nations, involved in their struggle for life and death with the Germans, Lenin was at that time merely a tool of their deadly foes. Ludendorff had dispatched Lenin to Russia in order to overthrow the Kerensky regime and to bring about the defection of Russia. The Bolshevists fought by force of arms all those Russians who wanted to continue the alliance with France, Great Britain and the United States. From a military point of view it was impossible for the Western nations to stay neutral while their Russian allies were desperately defending themselves against the Bolshevists. For the Allied Nations the Eastern Front was at stake. The cause of the "White" generals was their own cause.

As soon as the war against Germany came to an end in 1918, the Allies lost interest in Russian affairs. There was no longer any need for an Eastern Front. They did not care a whit about the internal problems of Russia. They longed for peace and were anxious to withdraw from the fighting. They were, of course, embarrassed because they did not know how to liquidate their venture with propriety. Their generals were ashamed of abandoning companions in arms who had fought to the best of their abilities in a common cause. To leave these men in the lurch was in their opinion nothing short of cowardice and desertion.

Such considerations of military honour delayed for some time the withdrawal of the inconspicuous Allied detachments and the termination of deliveries to the Whites. When this was finally accomplished, the Allied statesmen felt relief. From then on they adopted a policy of strict neutrality with regard to Russian affairs.

It was very unfortunate indeed that the Allied Nations had been willy nilly entangled in the Russian Civil War. It would have been better if the military situation of 1917 and 1918 had not compelled them to interfere. But one must not overlook the fact that the abandonment of intervention in Russia was tantamount to the final failure of President Wilson's policy. The United States had entered the war in order to make "the world safe for democracy." The victory had crushed the Kaiser and substituted in Germany a republican government for the comparatively mild and limited imperial autocracy. On the other hand, it had resulted in Russia in establishing a dictatorship compared with which the despotism of the Czars could be called liberal. But the Allies were not eager to make Russia safe for democracy as they had tried to do with Germany. After all, the Kaiser's Germany had parliaments, ministers responsible to the parliaments, trial by jury, freedom of thought, of religion and of the press not much more limited than in the West, and many other democratic institutions. But Soviet Russia was an unlimited despotism.

The Americans, the French and the British failed to see things from this angle. But the anti-democratic forces in Germany, Italy, Poland, Hungary and the Balkans thought differently. As the nationalists of these countries interpreted it, the neutrality of the Allied Powers with regard to Russia was evidence of the fact that their concern for democracy had been a mere blind. The

Allies, they argued, had fought Germany because they envied Germany's economic prosperity and they spared the new Russian autocracy because they were not afraid of Russian economic power. Democracy, these nationalists concluded, was nothing else than a convenient catchword to delude gullible people. And they became frightened that the emotional appeal of this slogan would one day be used as a disguise for insidious assaults against their own independence.

Since the abandonment of the intervention Russia had certainly no longer any reason to fear the great Western powers. Neither were the Soviets afraid of a Nazi aggression. The assertions to the contrary, very popular in Western Europe and in America, resulted from complete ignorance of German affairs. But the Russians knew Germany and the Nazis. They had read Mein Kampf. They learned from this book not only that Hitler coveted the Ukraine, but also that Hitler's fundamental strategical idea was to embark upon the conquest of Russia only after having definitely and forever annihilated France. The Russians were fully convinced that Hitler's expectation, as expressed in Mein Kampf, that Great Britain and the United States would keep out of this war and would quietly let France be destroyed, was vain. They were certain that such a new world war, in which they themselves planned to stay neutral, would result in a new German defeat. And this defeat, they argued, would make Germany—if not the whole of Europe— safe for Bolshevism. Guided by this opinion, Stalin already in the time of the Weimar Republic aided the then-secret German rearmament. The German communists helped the Nazis as much as they could in their endeavours to undermine the Weimar regime. Finally Stalin entered in August

1939 into an open alliance with Hitler, in order to give him a free hand against the West.

What Stalin—like all other people—did not anticipate was the overwhelming success of the German armies in 1940. Hitler attacked Russia in 1941 because he was fully convinced that not only France but also Great Britain was done for, and that the United States, menaced in the rear by Japan, would not be strong enough to interfere successfully with European affairs.

The disintegration of the Hapsburg Empire in 1918 and the Nazi defeat in 1945 have opened the gates of Europe to Russia. Russia is today the only military power on the European continent. But why are the Russians so intent upon conquering and annexing? They certainly do not need the resources of these countries. Neither is Stalin driven by the idea that such conquests could increase his popularity with the Russian masses. His subjects are indifferent to military glory.

It is not the masses whom Stalin wants to placate by his aggressive policy, but the intellectuals. For their Marxian orthodoxy is at stake, the very foundation of the Soviet might.

These Russian intellectuals were narrow-minded enough to absorb modifications of the Marxian creed which were in fact an abandonment of the essential teachings of dialectical materialism, provided that these modifications flattered their Russian chauvinism. They swallowed the doctrine that their holy Russia could skip one of the inextricable stages of economic evolution as described by Marx. They prided themselves on being the vanguard of the proletariat and the world revolution who, by realizing socialism first in one country only, set up a glorious example for all other nations. But it is impossible to explain to them why the other nations do not finally catch up with Russia. In the writings of Marx and Engels, which one cannot keep out of their hands, they discover that the fathers of Marxism considered Great Britain and France and even Germany as the countries most advanced in civilization and in the evolution of capitalism. These students of the Marxian universities may be too dull to comprehend the philosophical and economic doctrines of the Marxian gospel. But they are not too dull to see that Marx considered those Western countries as much more advanced than Russia.

Then some of these students of economic policies and statistics begin to suspect that the standard of living of the masses is much higher in the capitalist countries than in their own country. How can this be? Why are conditions much more propitious in the United States which—although foremost in capitalist production—is most backward in awakening class-consciousness in the proletarians?

The inference from these facts seems inescapable. If the most advanced countries do not adopt communism and fare rather well under capitalism, if communism is limited to a country which Marx considered as backward and does not bring about riches for all, is not perhaps the correct interpretation that communism is a feature of backward countries and results in general poverty? Must not a Russian patriot be ashamed of the fact that his country is committed to this system?

Such thoughts are very dangerous in a despotic country. Whoever dared to express them would be mercilessly liquidated by the G.P.U. But, even unspoken, they are on the tip of every intelligent man's tongue. They trouble the sleep of the supreme officials and perhaps even that of the great dictator.

He certainly has the power to crush every opponent. But considerations of expediency make it inadvisable to eradicate all somewhat judicious people and to run the country only with stupid blockheads.

This is the real crisis of Russian Marxism. Every day that passes without bringing the world revolution aggravates it. The Soviets must conquer the world or else they are menaced in their own country by a defection of the intelligentsia. It is concern about the ideological state of Russia's shrewdest minds that pushes Stalin's Russia towards unflinching aggression.

5. Trotsky's Heresy

The dictatorial doctrine as taught by the Russian Bolshevists, the Italian Fascists and the German Nazis tacitly implies that there cannot arise any disagreement with regard to the question who shall be the dictator. The mystical forces directing the course of historical events designate the providential leader. All righteous people are bound to submit to the unfathomable decrees of history and to bend their knees before the throne of the man of destiny. Those who decline to do so are heretics, abject scoundrels who must be "liquidated."

In reality the dictatorial power is seized by that candidate who succeeds in exterminating in time all his rivals and their helpers. The dictator paves his way to supreme power by slaughtering all his competitors. He preserves his eminent position by butchering all those who could possibly dispute it. The history of all oriental despotisms bears witness to this, as well as the experience of contemporary dictatorship.

When Lenin died in 1924, Stalin supplanted his most dangerous rival, Trotsky. Trotsky escaped, spent years abroad in various countries of Europe, Asia and America and was finally assassinated in Mexico City. Stalin remained the absolute ruler of Russia.

Trotsky was an intellectual of the orthodox Marxian type. As such he tried to represent his personal feud with Stalin as a conflict of principles. He tried to construct a Trotsky doctrine as distinguished from the Stalin doctrine. He branded Stalin's policies as an apostasy from the sacred legacy of Marx and Lenin. Stalin retorted in the same way. In fact, however, the conflict was a rivalry of two men, not a conflict of antagonistic ideas and principles. There was some minor dissent with regard to tactical methods. But in all essential matters Stalin and Trotsky were in agreement.

Trotsky had lived, before 1917, many years in foreign countries and was to some degree familiar with the main languages of the Western peoples. He posed as an expert in international affairs. Actually he did not know anything about Western civilization, political ideas and economic conditions. As a wandering exile he had moved almost exclusively in the circles of his fellow-exiles. The only foreigners whom he had met occasionally in coffee-houses and club-rooms of Western and Central Europe were radical doctrinaires, by their Marxian prepossessions precluded from reality. His main reading was Marxian books and periodicals. He scorned all other writings as "bourgeois" literature. He was absolutely unfitted to see events from any other angle than that of Marxism. Like Marx he was ready to interpret every great strike and every small riot as the sign of the outbreak of the final great revolution.

Stalin is a poorly educated Georgian. He has not the slightest knowledge of any Western language. He does not know Europe or America. Even his achievements as a Marxian author are questionable. But it was precisely the fact that, although an adamant supporter of communism, he was not indoctrinated with Marxian dogmas that made him superior to Trotsky. Stalin was not deluded by the spurious tenets of dialectical materialism. When faced with a problem, he did not search for an interpretation in the writings of Marx and Engels. He trusted his common sense. He was judicious enough to discern the fact that the policy of world revolution as inaugurated by Lenin and Trotsky in 1917 had failed completely outside the borders of Russia.

In Germany the communists, led by Karl Liebknecht and Rosa Luxemburg, were crushed by detachments of the regular army and by nationalist volunteers in a bloody battle fought in January 1919 in the streets of Berlin. The communist seizure of power in Munich in spring 1919 and the Hölz riot[29] in March 1921 ended likewise in disaster. In Hungary, in 1919, the communists were defeated by Horthy and Gömbös and the Rumanian army. In Austria various communist plots failed in 1918 and 1919; a violent upheaval in July 1927 was easily quelled by the Vienna police. In Italy, in 1920, the occupation of the factories was a complete miscarriage. In France and in Switzerland the

29 The Hölz riot was a communist uprising in Germany (March 1921 in Mansfeldischen), led by World War I veteran Max Hölz (1889-1933). Hölz was sentenced to life imprisonment as a result, granted amnesty in 1928, and then left Germany for the Soviet Union.

communist propaganda seemed to be very powerful in the first years following the Armistice of 1918; but it evaporated very soon. In Great Britain, in 1926, the general strike called by the labour unions resulted in lamentable failure.

Trotsky was so blinded by his orthodoxy that he refused to admit that the Bolshevist methods had failed. But Stalin realized it very well. He did not abandon the idea of instigating revolutionary outbreaks in all foreign countries and of conquering the whole world for the Soviets. But he was fully aware of the fact that it was necessary to postpone the aggression for a few years and to resort to new methods for its execution. Trotsky was wrong in accusing Stalin of strangling the communist movement outside of Russia. What Stalin really did was to apply other means for the attainment of ends which are common to him and all other Marxians.

As an exegetic of Marxian dogmas Stalin was certainly inferior to Trotsky. But he surpassed his rival by far as a politician. Bolshevism owes its successes in world policies to Stalin, not to Trotsky.

In the field of domestic policies, Trotsky resorted to the well-tried traditional tricks which Marxians had always applied in criticizing socialist measures adopted by other parties. Whatever Stalin did was not true socialism and communism, but, on the contrary, the very opposite of it, a monstrous perversion of the lofty principles of Marx and Lenin. All the disastrous features of public control of production and distribution as they appeared in Russia were, in Trotsky's interpretation, brought about by Stalin's policies. They were not unavoidable consequences of communist methods. They were attendant phenomena of Stalinism, not of communism. It was exclusively Stalin's fault that an absolutist irresponsible bureaucracy was supreme, that a class of privileged oligarchs enjoyed luxuries while the masses lived on the verge of starvation, that a terrorist regime executed the old guard of revolutionaries and condemned millions to slave labour in concentration camps, that the secret police was omnipotent, that the labour unions were powerless, that the masses were deprived of all rights and liberties. Stalin was not a champion of the egalitarian classless society. He was the pioneer of a return to the worst methods of class rule and exploitation. A new ruling class of about 10 percent of the population ruthlessly oppressed and exploited the immense majority of toiling proletarians.

Trotsky was at a loss to explain how all this could be achieved by only one man and his few sycophants. Where were the "material productive forces," much talked about in Marxian historical materialism, which—"independent of the wills of individuals"—determine the course of human events "with the inexorability of a law of nature"? How could it happen that one man was in a position to alter the "juridical and political superstructure" which is uniquely and inalterably fixed by the economic structure of society? Even Trotsky agreed that there was no longer any private ownership of the means of production in Russia. In Stalin's empire, production and distribution are entirely controlled by "society." It is a fundamental dogma of Marxism that the superstructure of such a system must necessarily be the bliss of the earthly paradise. There is in Marxian doctrines no room for an interpretation blaming individuals for a degenerative process which could convert the blessing of public control of business into evil. A consistent Marxian—if consistency were compatible with Marxism—would have to admit that Stalin's political system was the necessary superstructure of communism.

All essential items in Trotsky's programme were in perfect agreement with the policies of Stalin. Trotsky advocated the industrialization of Russia. It was this that Stalin's Five-Year Plans aimed at. Trotsky advocated the collectivization of agriculture. Stalin established the Kolkhoz and liquidated the Kulaks. Trotsky favoured the organization of a big army. Stalin organized such an army. Neither was Trotsky when still in power a friend of democracy. He was, on the contrary, a fanatical supporter of dictatorial oppression of all "saboteurs." It is true, he did not anticipate that the dictator could consider him, Trotsky, author of Marxian tracts and veteran of the glorious extermination of the Romanovs, as the most wicked saboteur. Like all other advocates of dictatorship, he assumed that he himself or one of his intimate friends would be the dictator.

Trotsky was a critic of bureaucratism. But he did not suggest any other method for the conduct of affairs in a socialist system. There is no other alternative to profit-seeking private business than bureaucratic management.[30]

The truth is that Trotsky found only one fault with Stalin: that he, Stalin, was the dictator and not himself, Trotsky. In their feud they both were right. Stalin was right in maintaining that his regime was the embodiment of socialist principles. Trotsky was right in asserting that Stalin's regime had made Russia a hell.

Trotskyism did not entirely disappear with Trotsky's death. Boulangerism in France, too, survived for some time the end of

---

30 Ludwig von Mises, *Bureaucracy* (Yale University Press, 1944).

General Boulanger. There are still Carlists left in Spain although the line of Don Carlos died out. Such posthumous movements are, of course, doomed.

But in all countries there are people who, although themselves fanatically committed to the idea of all-round planning, i.e. public ownership of the means of production, become frightened when they are confronted with the real face of communism. These people are disappointed. They dream of a Garden of Eden. For them communism, or socialism, means an easy life in riches and the full enjoyment of all liberties and pleasures. They fail to realize the contradictions inherent in their image of the communist society. They have uncritically swallowed all the lunatic fantasies of Charles Fourier and all the absurdities of Veblen. They firmly believe in Engels's assertion that socialism will be a realm of unlimited freedom. They indict capitalism for everything they dislike, and are fully convinced that socialism will deliver them from all evil. They ascribe their own failures and frustrations to the unfairness of this "mad" competitive system and expect that socialism will assign them that eminent position and high income which by right are due to them. They are Cinderellas yearning for the prince-saviour who will recognize their merits and virtues. The loathing of capitalism and the worship of communism are consolations for them. They help them to disguise to themselves their own inferiority, and to blame the "system" for their own shortcomings.

In advocating dictatorship such people always advocate the dictatorship of their own clique. In asking for planning, what they have in mind is always their own plan, not that of others. They will never admit that a socialist or communist regime is true and genuine socialism or communism, if it does not assign to themselves the most eminent position and the highest income. For them the essential feature of true and genuine communism is that all affairs are precisely conducted according to their own will, and that all those who disagree are beaten into submission.

It is a fact that the majority of our contemporaries are imbued with socialist and communist ideas. However, this does not mean that they are unanimous in their proposals for socialization of the means of production and public control of production and distribution. On the contrary. Each socialist coterie is fanatically opposed to the plans of all other socialist groups. The various socialist sects fight one another most bitterly.

If the case of Trotsky and the analogous case of Gregor Strasser in Nazi Germany were isolated cases, there would be no need to deal with them. But they are not casual incidents. They are typical. Study of them reveals the psychological causes both of the popularity of socialism and of its unfeasibility.

6. The Liberation of the Demons

The history of mankind is the history of ideas. For it is ideas, theories and doctrines that guide human action, determine the ultimate ends men aim at, and the choice of the means employed for the attainment of these ends. The sensational events which stir the emotions and catch the interest of superficial observers are merely the consummation of ideological changes. There are no such things as abrupt sweeping transformations of human affairs. What is called, in rather misleading terms, a "turning point in history" is the coming on the scene of forces which were already for a long time at work behind the scene. New ideologies, which had already long since superseded the old ones, throw off their last veil and even the dullest people become aware of the changes which they did not notice before.

In this sense Lenin's seizure of power in October 1917 was certainly a turning point. But its meaning was very different from that which the communists attribute to it.

The Soviet victory played only a minor role in the evolution towards socialism. The pro-socialist policies of the industrial countries of Central and Western Europe were of much greater consequence in this regard. Bismarck's social security scheme was a more momentous pioneering on the way towards socialism than was the expropriation of the backward Russian manufactures. The Prussian National Railways had provided the only instance of a government-operated business which, for some time at least, had avoided manifest financial failure. The British had already before 1914 adopted essential parts of the German social security system. In all industrial countries, the governments were committed to interventionist policies which were bound to result ultimately in socialism. During the war most of them embarked upon what was called war socialism. The German Hindenburg Programme which, of course, could not be executed completely on account of Germany's defeat, was no less radical but much better designed than the much talked about Russian Five-Year Plans.

For the socialists in the predominantly industrial countries of the West, the Russian methods could not be of any use. For these countries, production of manufactures for export was indispensable. They could not adopt the Russian system of economic autarky. Russia had never exported manufactures in quantities worth mentioning. Under the Soviet system it withdrew almost entirely from the world market of cereals and raw materials. Even fanatical socialists could not help admitting that the West could not learn anything from Russia. It is obvious that the technological achievements in which the Bolshevist gloried were merely clumsy imitations of things accomplished in the West. Lenin defined communism as: "the Soviet power plus electrification." Now, electrification was certainly not of Russian origin, and the Western nations surpass Russia in the field of electrification no less than in every other branch of industry.

The real significance of the Lenin revolution is to be seen in the fact that it was the bursting forth of the principle of unrestricted violence and oppression. It was the negation of all the political ideals that had for three thousand years guided the evolution of Western civilization.

State and government are the social apparatus of violent coercion and repression. Such an apparatus, the police power, is indispensable in order to prevent anti-social individuals and bands from destroying social co-operation. Violent prevention and suppression of anti-social activities benefit the whole of society and each of its members. But violence and oppression are none the less evils and corrupt those in charge of their application. It is necessary to restrict the power of those in office lest they become absolute despots. Society cannot exist without an apparatus of violent coercion. But neither can it exist if the office holders are irresponsible tyrants free to inflict harm upon those they dislike.

It is the social function of the laws to curb the arbitrariness of the police. The rule of law restricts the arbitrariness of the

Officers as much as possible. It strictly limits their discretion, and thus assigns to the citizens a sphere in which they are free to act without being frustrated by government interference.

Freedom and liberty always mean freedom from police interference. In nature there are no such things as liberty and freedom. There is only the adamant rigidity of the laws of nature to which man must unconditionally submit if he wants to attain any ends at all. Neither was there liberty in the imaginary paradisiacal conditions which, according to the fantastic prattle of many writers, preceded the establishment of societal bonds. Where there is no government, everybody is at the mercy of his stronger neighbour. Liberty can be realized only within an established state ready to prevent a gangster from killing and robbing his weaker fellows. But it is the rule of law alone which hinders the rulers from turning themselves into the worst gangsters.

The laws establish norms of legitimate action. They fix the procedures required for the repeal or alteration of existing laws and for the enactment of new laws. They likewise fix the procedures required for the application of the laws in definite cases, the due process of law. They establish courts and tribunals. Thus they are intent upon avoiding a situation in which the individuals are at the mercy of the rulers.

Mortal men are liable to error, and legislators and judges are mortal men. It may happen again and again that the valid laws or their interpretation by the courts prevent the executive organs from resorting to some measures which could be beneficial. No great harm, however, can result. If the legislators recognize the deficiency of the valid laws, they can alter them. It is certainly a bad thing that a criminal may sometimes evade punishment because there is a loophole left in the law, or because the prosecutor has neglected some formalities. But it is the minor evil when compared with the consequences of unlimited discretionary power on the part of the "benevolent" despot.

It is precisely this point which anti-social individuals fail to see. Such people condemn the formalism of the due process of law. Why should the laws hinder the government from resorting to beneficial measures? Is it not fetishism to make supreme the laws, and not expediency? They advocate the substitution of the welfare state (*Wohlfahrtsstaat*) for the state governed by the rule of law (Rechtsstaat). In this welfare state, paternal government should be free to accomplish all things it considers beneficial to the commonweal. No "scraps of paper" should restrain an enlightened ruler in his endeavours to promote the general welfare. All opponents must be crushed mercilessly lest they frustrate the beneficial action of the government. No empty formalities must protect them any longer against their well-deserved punishment.

It is customary to call the point of view of the advocates of the welfare state the "social" point of view as distinguished from the "individualistic" and "selfish" point of view of the champions of the rule of law. In fact, however, the supporters of the welfare state are utterly anti-social and intolerant zealots. For their ideology tacitly implies that the government will exactly execute what they themselves deem right and beneficial. They entirely disregard the possibility that there could arise disagreement with regard to the question of what is right and expedient and what is not. They advocate enlightened despotism, but they are convinced that the enlightened despot will in every detail comply with their own opinion concerning the measures to be adopted. They favour planning, but what they have in mind is exclusively their own plan, not those of other people. They want to exterminate all opponents, that is, all those who disagree with them. They are utterly intolerant and are not prepared to allow any discussion. Every advocate of the welfare state and of planning is a potential dictator. What he plans is to deprive all other men of all their rights, and to establish his own and his friends' unrestricted omnipotence. He refuses to convince his fellow-citizens. He prefers to "liquidate" them. He scorns the "bourgeois" society that worships law and legal procedure. He himself worships violence and bloodshed.

The irreconcilable conflict of these two doctrines, rule of law versus welfare state, was at issue in all the struggles which men fought for liberty. It was a long and hard evolution. Again and again the champions of absolutism triumphed. But finally the rule of law predominated in the realm of Western civilization. The rule of law, or limited government, as safeguarded by constitutions and bills of rights, is the characteristic mark of this civilization. It was the rule of law that brought about the marvelous achievements of modern capitalism and of its—as consistent Marxians should say—"superstructure," democracy. It secured for a steadily increasing population unprecedented well-being. The masses in the capitalist countries enjoy today a standard of living far above that of the well-to-do of earlier ages.

All these accomplishments have not restrained the advocates of despotism and planning. However, it would have been preposterous for the champions of totalitarianism to disclose the inextricable dictatorial consequences of their endeavours openly. In the nineteenth century the ideas of liberty and the rule of law had won such a prestige that it seemed crazy to attack them frankly. Public opinion was firmly convinced that despotism was done for and could never be restored. Was not even the Czar of barbarian Russia forced to abolish serfdom, to establish trial by jury, to grant a limited freedom to the press and to respect the laws?

Thus the socialists resorted to a trick. They continued to discuss the coming dictatorship of the proletariat, i.e., the dictatorship of each socialist author's own ideas, in their esoteric circles. But to the broad public they spoke in a different way. Socialism, they asserted, will bring true and full liberty and democracy. It will remove all kinds of compulsion and coercion. The state will "wither away." In the socialist commonwealth of the future there will be neither judges and policemen nor prisons and gallows.

But the Bolshevists took off the mask. They were fully convinced that the day of their final and unshakable victory had dawned. Further dissimulation was neither possible nor required. The gospel of bloodshed could be preached openly. It found an enthusiastic response among all the degenerate literati and parlour intellectuals who for many years already had raved about the writings of Sorel and Nietzsche. The fruits of the "treason of the intellectuals"[31] mellowed to maturity. The youths who had been fed on the ideas of Carlyle and Ruskin were ready to seize the reins.

Lenin was not the first usurper. Many tyrants had preceded

---

31 Julien Benda, *La trahison des clercs* (Paris, x927). Publisher's Note: In English, *The Treason of the Intellectuals* (New York: William Morrow, 1928) and *The Betrayal of the Intellectuals* (Boston: Beacon Press, 1955)

him. But his predecessors were in conflict with the ideas held by their most eminent contemporaries. They were opposed by public opinion because their principles of government were at variance with the accepted principles of right and legality. They were scorned and detested as usurpers. But Lenin's usurpation was seen in a different light. He was the brutal superman for whose coming the pseudo-philosophers had yearned. He was the counterfeit saviour whom history had elected to bring salvation through bloodshed. Was he not the most orthodox adept of Marxian "scientific" socialism? Was he not the man destined to realize the socialist plans for whose execution the weak statesmen of the decaying democracies were too timid? All well-intentioned people asked for socialism; science, through the mouths of the infallible professors, recommended it; the churches preached Christian socialism; the workers longed for the abolition of the wage system. Here was the man to fulfil all these wishes. He was judicious enough to know that you cannot make an omelet without breaking eggs.

Half a century ago all civilized people had censured Bismarck when he declared that history's great problems must be solved by blood and iron. Now the majority of quasi-civilized men bowed to the dictator who was prepared to shed much more blood than Bismarck ever did.

This was the true meaning of the Lenin revolution. All the traditional ideas of right and legality were overthrown. The rule of unrestrained violence and usurpation was substituted for the rule of law. The "narrow horizon of bourgeois legality," as Marx had dubbed it, was abandoned. Henceforth no laws could any longer limit the power of the elect. They were free to kill ad libitum. Man's innate impulses towards violent extermination of all whom he dislikes, repressed by a long and wearisome evolution, burst forth. The demons were unfettered. A new age, the age of the usurpers, dawned. The gangsters were called to action, and they listened to the Voice.

Of course, Lenin did not mean this. He did not want to concede to other people the prerogatives which he claimed for himself. He did not want to assign to other men the privilege of liquidating their adversaries. Him alone had history elected and entrusted with the dictatorial power. He was the only "legitimate" dictator because—an inner voice had told him so. Lenin was not bright enough to anticipate that other people, imbued with other creeds, could be bold enough to pretend that they also were called by an inner voice. Yet, within a few years too such men, Mussolini and Hitler, became quite conspicuous.

It is important to realize that Fascism and Nazism were socialist dictatorships. The communists, both the registered members of the communist parties and the fellow-travellers, stigmatize Fascism and Nazism as the highest and last and most depraved stage of capitalism. This is in perfect agreement with their habit of calling every party which does not unconditionally surrender to the dictates of Moscow—even the German Social Democrats, the classical party of Marxism—hirelings of capitalism.

It is of much greater consequence that the communists have succeeded in changing the semantic connotation of the term Fascism. Fascism, as will be shown later, was a variety of Italian socialism. It was adjusted to the particular conditions of the masses in overpopulated Italy. It was not a product of Mussolini's mind and will survive the fall of Mussolini. The foreign policies of Fascism and Nazism, from their early beginnings, were rather opposed to one another. The fact that the Nazis and the Fascists closely cooperated after the Ethiopian war, and were allies in the second World War, did not eradicate the differences between these two tenets any more than did the alliance between Russia and the United States eradicate the differences between Sovietism and the American economic system. Fascism and Nazism were both committed to the Soviet principle of dictatorship and violent oppression of dissenters. If one wants to assign Fascism and Nazism to the same class of political systems, one must call this class dictatorial regime and one must not neglect to assign the Soviets to the same class.

In recent years the communists' semantic innovations have gone even further. They call everybody whom they dislike, every advocate of the free enterprise system, a Fascist. Bolshevism, they say, is the only really democratic system. All non-communist countries and parties are essentially undemocratic and Fascist.

It is true that sometimes also non-socialists—the last vestiges of the old aristocracy—toyed with the idea of an aristocratic revolution modelled according to the pattern of Soviet dictatorship. Lenin had opened their eyes. What dupes, they moaned, have we been! We have let ourselves be deluded by the spurious catchwords of the liberal bourgeoisie. We believed that it was not permissible to deviate from the rule of law and to crush mercilessly those challenging our rights. How silly were these Romanovs in granting to their deadly foes the benefits of a fair legal trial! If somebody arouses the suspicion of Lenin, he is done for. Lenin does not hesitate to exterminate, without any trial, not only every suspect, but all his kin and friends too. But the Czars were superstitiously afraid of infringing the rules established by those scraps of paper called laws. When Alexander Ulyanov conspired against the Czar's life, he alone was executed; his brother Vladimir was spared. Thus Alexander III himself preserved the life of Ulyanov-Lenin, the man who ruthlessly exterminated his son, his daughter-in-law and their children and with them all the other members of the family he could catch. Was this not the most stupid and suicidal policy?

However, no action could result from the day dreams of these old Tories. They were a small group of powerless grumblers. They were not backed by any ideological forces and they had no followers.

The idea of such an aristocratic revolution motivated the German Stahlhelm and the French *Cagoulards*.[32] The Stahlhelm was simply dispelled by order of Hitler. The French Government could easily imprison the Cagoulards before they had any opportunity to do harm.

The nearest approach to an aristocratic dictatorship is Franco's regime. But Franco was merely a puppet of Mussolini and Hitler, who wanted to secure Spanish aid for the impending war against France or at least Spanish "friendly" neutrality. With his protectors gone, he will either have to adopt Western methods of government or face removal.

Dictatorship and violent oppression of all dissenters are today

---

32 Stahlhelm was an association of German World War veterans, established 1918. Cagoulards were members of a secret French extreme rightist, terrorist organization, the Cagoule. It was responsible for several assassinations of socialists and Italian anti-fascists and it collaborated with the Nazis and the French Vichy government during WWII (Pub.).

exclusively socialist institutions. This becomes clear as we take a closer look at Fascism and Nazism.

7. Fascism

When the war broke out in 1914, the Italian socialist party was divided as to the policy to be adopted.

One group clung to the rigid principles of Marxism. This war, they maintained, is a war of the capitalists. It is not seemly for the proletarians to side with any of the belligerent parties. The proletarians must wait for the great revolution, the civil war of the united socialists against the united exploiters. They must stand for Italian neutrality.

The second group was deeply affected by the traditional hatred of Austria. In their opinion the first task of the Italians was to free their unredeemed brethren. Only then would the day of the socialist revolution appear.

In this conflict Benito Mussolini, the outstanding man in Italian socialism, chose at first the orthodox Marxian position. Nobody could surpass Mussolini in Marxian zeal. He was the intransigent champion of the pure creed, the unyielding defender of the rights of the exploited proletarians, the eloquent prophet of the socialist bliss to come. He was an adamant adversary of patriotism, nationalism, imperialism, monarchical rule and all religious creeds. When Italy in 1911 opened the great series of wars by an insidious assault upon Turkey, Mussolini organized violent demonstrations against the departure of troops for Libya. Now, in 1914, he branded the war against Germany and Austria as an imperialist war. He was then still under the dominating influence of Angelica Balabanoff, the daughter of a wealthy Russian landowner. Miss Balabanoff had initiated him into the subtleties of Marxism. In her eyes the defeat of the Romanovs counted more than the defeat of the Habsburgs. She had no sympathy for the ideals of the Risorgimento.

But the Italian intellectuals were first of all nationalists. As in all other European countries, most of the Marxians longed for war and conquest. Mussolini was not prepared to lose his popularity. The thing he hated most was not to be on the side of the victorious faction. He changed his mind and became the most fanatical advocate of Italy's attack on Austria. With French financial aid he founded a newspaper to fight for the cause of the war.

The anti-Fascists blame Mussolini for this defection from the teachings of rigid Marxism. He was bribed, they say, by the French. Now, even these people should know that the publication of a newspaper requires funds. They themselves do not speak of bribery if a wealthy American provides a man with the money needed for the publication of a fellow-traveller newspaper, or if funds mysteriously flow into the communist publishing firms. It is a fact that Mussolini entered the scene of world politics as an ally of the democracies, while Lenin entered it as a virtual ally of imperial Germany.

More than anybody else Mussolini was instrumental in achieving Italy's entry into the first World War. His journalistic propaganda made it possible for the government to declare war on Austria. Only those few people have a right to find fault with his attitude in the years 1914 to 1918 who realize that the disintegration of the Austro-Hungarian Empire spelled the doom of Europe. Only those Italians are free to blame Mussolini who begin to understand that the only means of protecting the Italian-speaking minorities in the littoral districts of Austria against the threatening annihilation by the Slavonic majorities was to preserve the integrity of the Austrian state, whose constitution guaranteed equal rights to all linguistic groups. Mussolini was one of the most wretched figures of history. But the fact remains that his first great political deed still meets with the approval of all his countrymen and of the immense majority of his foreign detractors.

When the war came to an end, Mussolini's popularity dwindled. The communists, swept into popularity by events in Russia, carried on. But the great communist venture, the occupation of the factories in 1920, ended in complete failure, and the disappointed masses remembered the former leader of the socialist party. They flocked to Mussolini's new party, the Fascists. The youth greeted with turbulent enthusiasm the self-styled successor of the Caesars. Mussolini boasted in later years that he had saved Italy from the danger of communism. His foes passionately dispute his claims. Communism, they say, was no longer a real factor in Italy when Mussolini seized power. The truth is that the frustration of communism swelled the ranks of the Fascists and made it possible for them to destroy all other parties. The overwhelming victory of the Fascists was not the cause, but the consequence, of the communist fiasco.

The programme of the Fascists, as drafted in 1919, was vehemently anti-capitalistic.[33] The most radical New Dealers and

33 This program is reprinted in English in Count Carlo Sforza's book, *Contemporary Italy*, translated by Drake and Denise de Kay (New York, 1944), pp. 295-6.

even communists could agree with it. When the Fascists came to power, they had forgotten those points of their programme which referred to the liberty of thought and the press and the right of assembly. In this respect they were conscientious disciples of Bukharin and Lenin. Moreover they did not suppress, as they had promised, the industrial and financial corporations. Italy badly needed foreign credits for the development of its industries. The main problem for Fascism, in the first years of its rule, was to win the confidence of the foreign bankers. It would have been suicidal to destroy the Italian corporations.

Fascist economic policy did not—at the beginning—essentially differ from those of all other Western nations. It was a policy of interventionism. As the years went on, it more and more approached the Nazi pattern of socialism. When Italy, after the defeat of France, entered the second World War, its economy was by and large already shaped according to the Nazi pattern. The main difference was that the Fascists were less efficient and even more corrupt than the Nazis.

But Mussolini could not long remain without an economic philosophy of his own invention. Fascism posed as a new philosophy, unheard of before and unknown to all other nations. It claimed to be the gospel which the resurrected spirit of ancient Rome brought to the decaying democratic peoples whose barbarian ancestors had once destroyed the Roman empire. It was the consummation both of the Rinascimento and the Risorgimento in every respect, the final liberation of the Latin genius from the yoke of foreign ideologies. Its shining leader, the peerless Duce, was called to find the ultimate solution for the burning problems of society's economic organization and of social justice.

From the dust-heap of discarded socialist utopias, the Fascist scholars salvaged the scheme of guild socialism. Guild socialism was very popular with British socialists in the last years of the first World War and in the first years following the Armistice. It was so impracticable that it disappeared very soon from socialist literature. No serious statesman ever paid any attention to contradictory and confused plans of guild socialism. It was almost forgotten when the Fascists attached it to a new label, and flamboyantly proclaimed *corporativism* as the new social panacea. The public inside and outside of Italy was captivated. Innumerable books, pamphlets and articles were written in praise of the *stato corporativo*. The governments of Austria and Portugal very soon declared that they were committed to the noble principles of corporativism. The papal encyclical *Quadragesimo Anno* (1931) contained some paragraphs which could be interpreted—but need not be—as an approval of corporativism. In France its ideas found many eloquent supporters.

It was mere idle talk. Never did the Fascists make any attempt to realize the corporativist programme, industrial self-government. They changed the name of the chambers of commerce into corporative councils. They called *corporazione* the compulsory organizations of the various branches of industry which were the administrative units for the execution of the German pattern of socialism they had adopted. But there was no question of the *corporazione's* self-government. The Fascist cabinet did not tolerate anybody's interference with its absolute authoritarian control of production. All the plans for the establishment of the corporative system remained a dead letter.

Italy's main problem is its comparative overpopulation. In this age of barriers to trade and migration, the Italians are condemned to subsist permanently on a lower standard of living than that of the inhabitants of the countries more favoured by nature. The Fascists saw only one means to remedy this unfortunate situation: conquest. They were too narrow-minded to comprehend that the redress they recommended was spurious and worse than the evil. They were moreover so entirely blinded by self-conceit and vain-glory that they failed to realize that their provocative speeches were simply ridiculous. The foreigners whom they insolently challenged knew very well how negligible Italy's military forces were.

Fascism was not, as its advocates boasted, an original product of the Italian mind. It began with a split in the ranks of Marxian socialism, which certainly was an imported doctrine. Its economic programme was borrowed from German non-Marxian socialism and its aggressiveness was likewise copied from Germans, the *All-deutsche* or Pan-German forerunners of the Nazis. Its conduct of government affairs was a replica of Lenin's dictatorship. Corporativism, its much advertised ideological adornment, was of British origin. The only home-grown ingredient of Fascism was the theatrical style of its processions, shows and festivals.

The short lived Fascist episode ended in blood, misery and ignominy. But the forces which generated Fascism are not dead. Fanatical nationalism is a feature common to all present-day Italians. The communists are certainly not prepared to renounce their principle of dictatorial oppression of all dissenters. Neither do the Catholic parties advocate freedom of thought, of the press or of religion. There are in Italy only very few people indeed who comprehend that the indispensable prerequisite of democracy and the rights of men is economic freedom.

It may happen that Fascism will be resurrected under a new label and with new slogans and symbols. But if this happens, the consequences will be detrimental. For Fascism is not as the Fascists trumpeted a "new way to life,"[34] it is a rather old way towards destruction and death.

8. Nazism

The philosophy of the Nazis, the *German National Socialist Labour Party*, is the purest and most consistent manifestation of the anticapitalistic and socialistic spirit of our age. Its essential ideas are not German or "Aryan" in origin, nor are they peculiar to the present day Germans. In the genealogical tree of the Nazi doctrine such Latins as Sismondi and Georges Sorel, and such Anglo-Saxons as Carlyle, Ruskin and Houston Stewart Chamberlain, were more conspicuous than any German. Even the best known ideological attire of Nazism, the fable of the superiority of the Aryan master race, was not of German provenance; its author was a Frenchman, Gobineau. Germans of Jewish descent, like Lassalle, Lasson, Stahl and Walter Rathenau, contributed more to the essential tenets of Nazism than such men as Sombart, Spann and Ferdinand Fried. The slogan into which the Nazis condensed their economic philosophy, viz., *Gemeinnutz geht vor Eigennutz* (i.e., the commonweal ranks above private profit), is likewise the idea underlying the American New Deal

---

34 For instance Mario Palmieri, *The Philosophy of Fascism* (Chicago, 1936), p. 248.

and the Soviet management of economic affairs. It implies that profit-seeking business harms the vital interests of the immense majority, and that it is the sacred duty of popular government to prevent the emergence of profits by public control of production and distribution.

The only specifically German ingredient in Nazism was its striving after the conquest of *Lebensraum*. And this, too, was an outcome of their agreement with the ideas guiding the policies of the most influential political parties of all other countries. These parties proclaim income equality as the main thing. The Nazis do the same. What characterizes the Nazis is the fact that they are not prepared to acquiesce in a state of affairs in which the Germans are doomed forever to be "imprisoned," as they say, in a comparatively small and overpopulated area in which the productivity of labour must be smaller than in the comparatively underpopulated countries, which are better endowed with natural resources and capital goods. They aim at a fairer distribution of earth's natural resources. As a "have-not" nation they look at the wealth of the richer nations with the same feelings with which many people in the Western countries look at the higher incomes of some of their countrymen. The "progressives" in the Anglo-Saxon countries assert that "liberty is not worth having" for those who are wronged by the comparative smallness of their incomes. The Nazis say the same with regard to international relations. In their opinion the only freedom that matters is *Nahrungsfreiheit* (viz., freedom from importing food). They aim at the acquisition of a territory so large and rich in natural resources that they could live in economic self-sufficiency at a standard not lower than that of any other nation. They consider themselves as revolutionaries fighting for their inalienable natural rights against the vested interests of a host of reactionary nations.

It is easy for economists to explode the fallacies involved in the Nazi doctrines. But those who disparage economics as "orthodox and reactionary," and fanatically support the spurious creeds of socialism and economic nationalism, were at a loss to refute them. For Nazism was nothing but the logical application of their own tenets to the particular conditions of comparatively overpopulated Germany.

For more than seventy years the German professors of political science, history, law, geography and philosophy eagerly imbued their disciples with a hysterical hatred of capitalism, and preached the war of "liberation" against the capitalistic West. The German "socialists of the chair," much admired in all foreign countries, were the peacemakers of the two World Wars. At the turn of the century the immense majority of the Germans were already radical supporters of socialism and aggressive nationalism. They were then already firmly committed to the principles of Nazism. What was lacking and was added later was only a new term to signify their doctrine.

When the Soviet policies of mass extermination of all dissenters and of ruthless violence removed the inhibitions against wholesale murder, which still troubled some of the Germans, nothing could any longer stop the advance of Nazism. The Nazis were quick to adopt the Soviet methods. They imported from Russia: the one-party system and the pre-eminence of this party in political life; the paramount position assigned to the secret police; the concentration camps; the administrative execution or imprisonment of all opponents; the extermination of the families of suspects and of exiles; the methods of propaganda; the organization of affiliated parties abroad and their employment for fighting their domestic governments and espionage and sabotage; the use of the diplomatic and consular service for fomenting revolution; and many other things besides. There were nowhere more docile disciples of Lenin, Trotsky and Stalin than the Nazis were.

Hitler was not the founder of Nazism; he was its product. He was, like most of his collaborators, a sadistic gangster. He was uneducated and ignorant; he had failed even in the lower grades of high school. He never had any honest job. It is a fable that he had ever been a paperhanger. His military career in the first World War was rather mediocre. The First Class Iron Cross was given to him after the end of the war as a reward for his activities as a political agent. He was a maniac obsessed by megalomania. But learned professors nourished his self-conceit. Werner Sombart, who once had boasted that his life was devoted to the task of fighting for the ideas of Marx, [35]Sombart, whom the American Economic Association had elected to Honorary membership and many non-German universities to honorary degrees, candidly declared that Führertum means a permanent revelation and that the Führer received his orders directly from God, the supreme Führer of the Universe.[36]

The Nazi plan was more comprehensive and therefore more pernicious than that of the Marxians. It aimed at abolishing

35 Werner Sombart, *Das Lebenswerk yon Karl Marx* (Jena, 1909), p. 3.

36 Werner Sombart, *A New Social Philosophy*, trans. and ed. K. F. Geiser (Princeton University Press, 1937), p. 194

laissez-faire not only in the production of material goods, but no less in the production of men. The Führer was not only the general manager of all industries; he was also the general manager of the breeding farm intent upon rearing superior men and eliminating inferior stock. A grandiose scheme of eugenics was to be put into effect according to "scientific" principles.

It is vain for the champions of eugenics to protest that they did not mean what the Nazis executed. Eugenics aims at placing some men, backed by the police power, in complete control of human reproduction. It suggests that the methods applied to domestic animals be applied to men. This is precisely what the Nazis tried to do. The only objection which a consistent eugenist can raise is that his own plan differs from that of the Nazi scholars and that he wants to rear another type of men than the Nazis. As every supporter of economic planning aims at the execution of his own plan only, so every advocate of eugenic planning aims at the execution of his own plan and wants himself to act as the breeder of human stock.

The eugenists pretend that they want to eliminate criminal individuals. But the qualification of a man as a criminal depends upon the prevailing laws of the country and varies with the change in social and political ideologies. John Huss, Giordano Bruno and Galileo Galilei were criminals from the point of view of the laws which their judges applied. When Stalin robbed the Russian State Bank of several million rubles, he committed a crime. Today it is an offence in Russia to disagree with Stalin. In Nazi Germany sexual intercourse between "Aryans" and the members of an "inferior" race was a crime. Whom do the eugenists want to eliminate, Brutus or Caesar? Both violated the laws of their country. If eighteenth-century eugenists had prevented alcohol addicts from generating children, their planning would have eliminated Beethoven.

It must be emphasized again: there is no such thing as a scientific ought. Which men are superior and which are inferior can only be decided by personal value judgments not liable to Verification or falsification. The eugenists delude themselves in assuming that they themselves will be called to decide what qualities are to be conserved in the human stock. They are too dull to take into account the possibility that other people might make the choice according to their own value judgments.[37] In the eyes of the Nazis the brutal killer, the "fair-haired beast," is the most perfect specimen of mankind.

The mass slaughters perpetrated in the Nazi horror camps are too horrible to be adequately described by words. But they were the logical and consistent application of doctrines and policies parading as applied science and proved by some men who in a sector of the natural sciences have displayed acumen and technical skill in laboratory research.

9. The Teachings of Soviet Experience

Many people all over the world assert that the Soviet "experiment" has supplied conclusive evidence in favour of socialism and disproved all, or at least most, of the objections raised against it. The facts, they say, speak for themselves. It is no

37 The devastating critique of eugenics by H. S. Jennings, *The Biological Basis of Human Nature* (New York, 1930), pp. 223-52.

longer permissible to pay any attention to the spurious aprioristic reasoning of armchair economists criticizing the socialist plans. A crucial experiment has exploded their fallacies.

It is, first of all, necessary to comprehend that in the field of purposive human action and social relations no experiments can be made and no experiments have ever been made. The experimental method to which the natural sciences owe all their achievements is inapplicable in the social sciences. The natural sciences are in a position to observe in the laboratory experiment the consequences of the isolated change in one element only, while other elements remain unchanged. Their experimental observation refers ultimately to certain isolable elements in sense experience. What the natural sciences call facts are the causal relations shown in such experiments. Their theories and hypotheses must be in agreement with these facts.

But the experience with which the sciences of human action have to deal is essentially different. It is historical experience. It is an experience of complex phenomena, of the joint effects brought about by the cooperation of a multiplicity of elements. The social sciences are never in a position to control the conditions of change and to isolate them from one another in the way in which the experimenter proceeds in arranging his experiments. They never enjoy the advantage of observing the consequences of a change in one element only, other conditions being equal. They are never faced with facts in the sense in which the natural sciences employ this term. Every fact and every experience with which the social sciences have to deal is open to various interpretations. Historical facts and historical experience can never prove or disprove a statement in the way in which an experiment proves or disproves.

Historical experience never comments upon itself. It needs to be interpreted from the point of view of theories constructed without the aid of experimental observations. There is no need to enter into an epistemological analysis of the logical and philosophical problems involved. It is enough to refer to the fact that nobody—whether scientist or layman--ever proceeds otherwise when dealing with historical experience. Every discussion of the relevance and meaning of historical facts falls back very soon on a discussion of abstract general principles, logically antecedent to the facts to be elucidated and interpreted. Reference to historical experience can never solve any problem or answer any question. The same historical events and the same statistical figures are claimed as confirmations of contradictory theories.

If history could prove and teach us anything, it would be that private ownership of the means of production is a necessary requisite of civilization and material well-being. All civilizations have up to now been based on private property. Only nations committed to the principle of private property have risen above penury and produced science, art and literature. There is no experience to show that any other social system could provide mankind with any of the achievements of civilization. Nevertheless, only few people consider this as a sufficient and incontestable refutation of the socialist programme.

On the contrary, there are even people who argue the other way round. It is frequently asserted that the system of private property is done for precisely because it was the system that men applied in the past. However beneficial a social system may have been in the past, they say, it cannot be so in the future too; a new age requires a new mode of social organization. Mankind has reached maturity; it would be pernicious for it to cling to the principles to which it resorted in the earlier stages of its evolution. This is certainly the most radical abandonment of experimentalism. The experimental method may assert: because a produced in the past the result b, it will produce it in the future also. It must never assert because a produced in the past the result b, it is proved that it cannot produce it any longer.

In spite of the fact that mankind has had no experience with the socialist mode of production, the socialist writers have constructed various schemes of socialist systems based on aprioristic reasoning. But as soon as anybody dares to analyse these projects and to scrutinize them with regard to their feasibility and their ability to further human welfare, the socialists vehemently object. These analyses, they say, are merely idle aprioristic speculations. They cannot disprove the correctness of our statements and the expediency of our plans. They are not experimental. One must try socialism and then the results will speak for themselves.

What these socialists ask for is absurd. Carried to its ultimate logical consequences, their idea implies that men are not free to refute by reasoning any scheme, however nonsensical, self-contradictory and impracticable, that any reformer is pleased to suggest. According to their view, the only method permissible for the refutation of such a—necessarily abstract and aprioristic—plan is to test it by reorganizing the whole of society according to its designs. As soon as a man sketches the plan for a better social order, all nations are bound to try it and to see what will happen.

Even the most stubborn socialists cannot fail to admit that there are various plans for the construction of the future utopia, incompatible with one another. There is the Soviet pattern of all-round socialization of all enterprises and their outright bureaucratic management; there is the German pattern of Zwangswirtschaft, towards the complete adoption of which the Anglo-Saxon countries are manifestly tending; there is guild socialism, under the name of corporativism still very popular in some Catholic countries. There are many other varieties. The supporters of most of these competing schemes assert that the beneficial results to be expected from their own scheme will appear only when all nations will have adopted it; they deny that socialism in one country only can already bring the blessings they ascribe to socialism. The Marxians declare that the bliss of socialism will emerge only in its "higher phase" which, as they hint, will appear only after the working class will have passed "through long struggles, through a whole series of historical processes, wholly transforming both circumstances and men."[38] The inference from all this is that one must realize socialism and quietly wait for a very long time until its promised benefits come. No unpleasant experiences in the period of transition, no matter how long this period may be, can disprove the assertion that socialism is the best of all conceivable modes of social organization. He that believeth shall be saved.

But which of the many socialist plans, contradicting one another, should be adopted? Every socialist sect passionately proclaims that its own brand is alone genuine socialism and that all other sects advocate counterfeit, entirely pernicious measures. In fighting one another, the various socialist factions resort to

---

38 Karl Marx, *Der Bürgerkrieg in Frankreich*, ed. Pfemfert (Berlin, 1919), p. 54. Publisher's Note: In English, "The Civil War in France," p. 408.

the same methods of abstract reasoning which they stigmatize as vain apriorism whenever they are applied against the correctness of their own statements and the expediency and practicability of their own schemes. There is, of course, no other method available. The fallacies implied in a system of abstract reasoning—such as socialism is—cannot be smashed otherwise than by abstract reasoning.

The fundamental objection advanced against the practicability of socialism refers to the impossibility of economic calculation. It has been demonstrated in an irrefutable way that a socialist commonwealth would not be in a position to apply economic calculation. Where there are no market prices for the factors of production because they are neither bought nor sold, it is impossible to resort to calculation in planning future action and in determining the result of past action. A socialist management of production would simply not know whether or not what it plans and executes is the most appropriate means to attain the ends sought. It will operate in the dark, as it were. It will squander the scarce factors of production both material and human (labour). Chaos and poverty for all will unavoidably result.

All earlier socialists were too narrow-minded to see this essential point. Neither did the earlier economists conceive its full importance. When the present writer in 1920 showed the impossibility of economic calculation under socialism, the apologists of socialism embarked upon the search for a method of calculation applicable to a socialist system. They utterly failed in these endeavours. The futility of the schemes they produced could easily be shown. Those communists who were not entirely intimidated by the fear of the Soviet executioners, for instance

Trotsky, freely admitted that economic accounting is unthinkable without market relations.[39] The intellectual bankruptcy of the socialist doctrine can no longer be disguised. In spite of its unprecedented popularity, socialism is done for. No economist can any longer question its impracticability. The avowal of socialist ideas is today the proof of a complete ignorance of the basic problems of economics. The socialist's claims are as vain as those of the astrologers and the magicians.

With regard to this essential problem of socialism, viz., economic calculation, the Russian "experiment" is of no avail. The Soviets are operating within a world the greater part of which still clings to a market economy. They base the calculations on which they make their decisions on the prices established abroad. Without the help of these prices their actions would be aimless and planless. Only as far as they refer to this foreign price system are they able to calculate, keep books and prepare their plans. In this respect one may agree with the statement of various socialist and communist authors that socialism in one or a few countries only is not yet true socialism. Of course, these authors attach a quite different meaning to their assertion. They want to say that the full blessings of socialism can be reaped only in a world-embracing socialist community. Those familiar with the teachings of economics must, on the contrary, recognize that socialism will result in full chaos precisely if it is applied in the greater part of the world.

The second main objection raised against socialism is that

---

39 F. A. Hayek, *Individualism and the Economic Order* (Chicago University Press, 1948), pp. 89-91

it is a less efficient mode of production than is capitalism and that it will impair the productivity of labour. Consequently, in a socialist commonwealth the standard of living of the masses will be low when compared with conditions prevailing under capitalism. There is no doubt that this objection has not been disproved by the Soviet experience. The only certain fact about Russian affairs under the Soviet regime with regard to which all people agree is: that the standard of living of the Russian masses is much lower than that of the masses in the country which is universally considered as the paragon of capitalism, the United States of America. If we were to regard the Soviet regime as an experiment, we would have to say that the experiment has clearly demonstrated the superiority of capitalism and the inferiority of socialism.

It is true that the advocates of socialism are intent upon interpreting the lowness of the Russian standard of living in a different way. As they see things, it was not caused by socialism, but was—in spite of socialism—brought about by other agencies. They refer to various factors, e.g., the poverty of Russia under the Czars, the disastrous effects of the wars, the alleged hostility of the capitalist democratic nations, the alleged sabotage of the remnants of the Russian aristocracy and bourgeoisie and of the Kulaks. There is no need to enter into an examination of these matters. For we do not contend that any historical experience could prove or disprove a theoretical statement in the way in which a crucial experiment can verify or falsify a statement concerning natural events. It is not the critics of socialism, but its fanatical advocates, who maintain that the Soviet "experiment" proves something with regard to the effects of socialism. However, what they are really doing in dealing with the manifest and undisputed facts of Russian experience is to push them aside by impermissible tricks and fallacious syllogisms. They disavow the obvious facts by commenting upon them in such a way as to deny their bearing and their significance upon the question to be answered.

Let us, for the sake of argument, assume that their interpretation is correct. But then it would still be absurd to assert that the Soviet experiment has evidenced the superiority of socialism. All that could be said is: the fact that the masses' standard of living is low in Russia does not provide conclusive evidence that socialism is inferior to capitalism.

A comparison with experimentation in the field of the natural sciences may clarify the issue. A biologist wants to test a new patent food. He feeds it to a number of guinea pigs. They all lose weight and finally die. The experimenter believes that their decline and death were not caused by the patent food, but by merely accidental affliction with pneumonia. It would nevertheless be absurd for him to proclaim that his experiment had evidenced the nutritive value of the compound because the unfavourable result is to be ascribed to accidental occurrences, not causally linked with the experimental arrangement. The best he could contend is that the outcome of the experiment was not conclusive, that it does not prove anything against the nutritive value of the food tested. Things are, he could assert, as if no experiment had been tried at all.

Even if the Russian masses' standard of living were much higher than that of the capitalist countries, this still would not be conclusive proof of the superiority of socialism. It may be admitted that the undisputed fact that the standard of living in

Russia is lower than that in the capitalist West does not conclusively prove the inferiority of socialism. But it is nothing short of idiocy to announce that the experience of Russia has demonstrated the superiority of public control of production.

Neither does the fact that the Russian armies, after having suffered many defeats, finally—with armament manufactured by American big business and donated to them by the American taxpayers—could aid the Americans in the conquest of Germany prove the pre-eminence of communism. When the British forces had to sustain a temporary reverse in North Africa, Professor Harold Laski, that most radical advocate of socialism, was quick to announce the final failure of capitalism. He was not consistent enough to interpret the German conquest of the Ukraine as the final failure of Russian communism. Neither did he retract his condemnation of the British system when his country emerged victorious from the war. If the military events are to be considered as the proof of any social system's excellence, it is rather the American than the Russian system for which they bear witness.

Nothing that has happened in Russia since 1917 contradicts any of the statements of the critics of socialism and communism. Even if one bases one's judgment exclusively on the writings of communists and fellow-travellers, one cannot discover any feature in Russian conditions that tells in favour of the Soviet's social and political system. All the technological improvements of the last decades originated in the capitalistic countries. It is true that the Russians have tried to copy some of these innovations. But so did all backward oriental peoples too.

Some communists are eager to have us believe that the ruthless oppression of dissenters and the radical abolition of the freedom of thought, speech and the press are not inherent marks of the public control of business. They are, they argue, only accidental phenomena of communism, its signature in a country which—as was the case with Russia—never enjoyed freedom of thought and conscience. However, these apologists for totalitarian despotism are at a loss to explain how the rights of man could be safeguarded under government omnipotence.

Freedom of thought and conscience is a sham in a country in which the authorities are free to exile everybody whom they dislike into the Arctic or the desert, and to assign him hard labour for life. The autocrat may always try to justify such arbitrary acts by pretending that they are motivated exclusively by considerations of public welfare and economic expediency. He alone is the supreme arbiter to decide all matters referring to the execution of the plan. Freedom of the press is illusory when the government owns and operates all paper mills, printing offices and publishing houses, and ultimately decides what is to be printed and what not. The right of assembly is vain if the government owns all assembly halls and determines for what purposes they shall be used. And so it is with all other liberties too. In one of his lucid intervals Trotsky—of course Trotsky the hunted exile, not the ruthless commander of the Red army—saw things realistically and declared: "In a country where the sole employer is the State, opposition means death by slow starvation. The old principle: who does not work shall not eat, has been replaced by a new one: who does not obey shall not eat."[40] This confession settles the issue.

---

40 Quoted by F. A. Hayek, *The Road to Serfdom* (1944), Chapter IX, p. 119.

What the Russian experience shows is a very low level of the standard of living of the masses and unlimited dictatorial despotism. The apologists of communism are intent upon explaining these uncontested facts as accidental only; they are, they say, not the fruit of communism, but occurred in spite of communism. But even if one were to accept these excuses for the sake of argument, it would be nonsensical to maintain that the Soviet "experiment" has demonstrated anything in favour of communism and socialism.

10. The Alleged Inevitability of Socialism

Many people believe that the coming of totalitarianism is inevitable. The "wave of the future," they say, "carries mankind inexorably towards a system under which all human affairs are managed by omnipotent dictators. It is useless to fight against the unfathomable decrees of history."

The truth is that most people lack the intellectual ability and courage to resist a popular movement, however pernicious and ill-considered. Bismarck once deplored the lack of what he called civilian courage, i.e., bravery in dealing with civic affairs, on the part of his countrymen. But neither did the citizens of other nations display more courage and judiciousness when faced with the menace of communist dictatorship. They either yielded silently, or timidly raised some trifling objections.

One does not fight socialism by criticizing only some accidental features of its schemes. In attacking many socialists' stand on divorce and birth control, or their ideas about art and literature, one does not refute socialism. It is not enough to disapprove of the Marxian assertions that the theory of relativity or the philosophy of Bergson or psycho-analysis is "bourgeois" moonshine. Those who find fault with Bolshevism and Nazism only for their anti-Christian leanings implicitly endorse all the rest of these bloody schemes.

On the other hand, it is sheer stupidity to praise the totalitarian regimes for alleged achievements which have no reference whatever to their political and economic principles. It is questionable whether the observations that in Fascist Italy the railway trains ran on schedule and the bug population of second-rate hotel beds was decreasing, were correct or not; but it is in any case of no importance for the problem of Fascism. The fellow-travellers are enraptured by Russian films, Russian music and Russian caviar. But there lived greater musicians in other countries and under other social systems; good pictures were produced in other countries too; and it is certainly not a merit of Generalissimo Stalin that the taste of caviar is delicious. Neither does the prettiness of Russian ballet dancers or the construction of a great power station on the Dnieper expiate for the mass slaughter of the Kulaks.

The readers of picture magazines and the movie-fans long for the picturesque. The operatic pageants of the Fascists and the Nazis and the parading of the girl-battalions of the Red Army are after their heart. It is more fun to listen to the radio speeches of a dictator than to study economic treatises. The entrepreneurs and technologists who pave the way for economic improvement work in seclusion; their work is not suitable to be visualized on the screen. But the dictators, intent upon spreading death and destruction, are spectacularly in sight of the public. Dressed in military garb they eclipse in the eyes of the movie-goers the colourless bourgeois in plain clothes.

The problems of society's economic organization are not suitable for light talk at fashionable cocktail parties. Neither can they be dealt with adequately by demagogues haranguing mass assemblies. They are serious things. They require painstaking study. They must not be taken lightly.

The socialist propaganda never encountered any decided opposition. The devastating critique by which the economists exploded the futility and impracticability of the socialist schemes and doctrines did not reach the moulders of public opinion. The universities were mostly dominated by socialist or interventionist pedants not only in continental Europe, where they were owned and operated by the governments, but even in the Anglo-Saxon countries. The politicians and the statesmen, anxious not to lose popularity, were lukewarm in their defence of freedom. The policy of appeasement, so much criticized when applied in the case of the Nazis and the Fascists, was practised universally for many decades with regard to all other brands of socialism. It was this defeatism that made the rising generation believe that the victory of socialism is inevitable.

It is not true that the masses are vehemently asking for socialism and that there is no means to resist them. The masses favour socialism because they trust the socialist propaganda of the intellectuals. The intellectuals, not the populace, are moulding public opinion. It is a lame excuse of the intellectuals that they must yield to the masses. They themselves have generated the socialist ideas and indoctrinated the masses with them. No proletarian or son of a proletarian has contributed to the elaboration of the interventionist and socialist programmes. Their authors were all of bourgeois background. The esoteric writings of dialectical materialism, of Hegel, the father both of Marxism and of German aggressive nationalism, the books of Georges Sorel, of Gentile and of Spengler were not read by the average man; they did not move the masses directly. It was the intellectuals who popularized them.

The intellectual leaders of the peoples have produced and propagated the fallacies which are on the point of destroying liberty and Western civilization. The intellectuals alone are responsible for the mass slaughters which are the characteristic mark of our century. They alone can reverse the trend and pave the way for a resurrection of freedom.

Not mythical "material productive forces," but reason and ideas determine the course of human affairs. What is needed to stop the trend towards socialism and despotism is common sense and moral courage.

PROFIT AND LOSS

This essay was originally presented at the Mont Pelerin meeting, Beauvallon, France, in September 1951, and was published in *Planning for Freedom* in 1952.

A. The Economic Nature of Profit and Loss

1. The Emergence of Profit and Loss

In the capitalist system of society's economic organization the entrepreneurs determine the course of production. In the performance of this function they are unconditionally and totally subject to the sovereignty of the buying public, the consumers. If they fail to produce in the cheapest and best possible way those commodities which the consumers are asking for most urgently, they suffer losses and are finally eliminated from their entrepreneurial position. Other men who know better how to serve the consumers replace them.

If all people were to anticipate correctly the future state of the market, the entrepreneurs would neither earn any profits nor suffer any losses. They would have to buy the complementary factors of production at prices which would, already at the instant of the purchase, fully reflect the future prices of the products. No room would be left either for profit or for loss. What makes profit emerge is the fact that the entrepreneur who judges the future prices of the products more correctly than other people do buys some or all of the factors of production at prices which, seen from the point of view of the future state of the market, are too low. Thus the total costs of production — including interest on the capital invested — lag behind the prices which the entrepreneur receives for the product. This difference is entrepreneurial profit.

On the other hand, the entrepreneur who misjudges the future prices of the products allows for the factors of production prices which, seen from the point of view of the future state of the market, are too high. His total costs of production exceed the prices at which he can sell the product. This difference is entrepreneurial loss.

Thus profit and loss are generated by success or failure in adjusting the course of production activities to the most urgent demand of the consumers. Once this adjustment is achieved, they disappear. The prices of the complementary factors of production reach a height at which total costs of production coincide with the price of the product. Profit and loss are ever-present features only on account of the fact that ceaseless change in the economic data makes again and again new discrepancies, and consequently the need for new adjustments originate.

2. The Distinction Between Profits and Other Proceeds

Many errors concerning the nature of profit and loss were caused by the practice of applying the term profit to the totality of the residual proceeds of an entrepreneur.

Interest on the capital employed is not a component part of profit. The dividends of a corporation are not profit. They are interest on the capital invested plus profit or minus loss.

The market equivalent of work performed by the entrepreneur in the conduct of the enterprise's affairs is entrepreneurial quasi-wages but not profit.

If the enterprise owns a factor on which it can earn monopoly prices, it makes a monopoly gain. If this enterprise is a corporation, such gains increase the dividend. Yet they are not profit proper. Still more serious are the errors due to the confusion of entrepreneurial activity and technological innovation and improvement.

The maladjustment the removal of which is the essential function of entrepreneurship may often consist in the fact that new technological methods have not yet been utilized to the full extent to which they should be in order to bring about the best possible satisfaction of consumers' demand. But this is not necessarily always the case. Changes in the data, especially in consumers' demand, may require adjustments which have no reference at all to technological innovations and improvements. The entrepreneur who simply increases the production of an article by adding to the existing production facilities a new outfit without any change in the technological method of production is no less an entrepreneur than the man who inaugurates a new way of producing. The business of the entrepreneur is not merely to experiment with new technological methods, but to select from the multitude of technologically feasible methods those which are best fit to supply the public in the cheapest way with the things they are asking for most urgently. Whether a new technological procedure is or is not fit for this purpose is to be provisionally decided by the entrepreneur and will be finally decided by the conduct of the buying public. The question is not whether a new method is to be considered as a more "elegant" solution of a technological problem. It is whether, under the given state of economic data, it is the best possible method of supplying the consumers in the cheapest way.

The activities of the entrepreneur consist in making decisions. He determines for what purpose the factors of production should be employed. Any other acts which an entrepreneur may perform are merely accidental to his entrepreneurial function. It is this that laymen often fail to realize. They confuse the entrepreneurial activities with the conduct of the technological and administrative affairs of a plant. In their eyes not the stockholders, the promoters and speculators, but hired employees are the real entrepreneurs. The former are merely idle parasites who pocket the dividends.

Now nobody ever contended that one could produce without working. But neither is it possible to produce without capital goods, the previously produced factors of further production. These capital goods are scarce, i.e., they do not suffice for the production of all things which one would like to have produced. Hence the economic problem arises: to employ them in such a way that only those goods should be produced which are fit to satisfy the most urgent demands of the consumers. No good should remain unproduced on account of the fact that the factors required for its production were used — wasted — for the production of another good for which the demand of the public is less intense. To achieve this is under capitalism the function of entrepreneurship that determines the allocation of capital to the various branches of production.

Under socialism it would be a function of the state, the social apparatus of coercion and oppression. The problem whether a socialist directorate, lacking any method of economic calculation, could fulfill this function is not to be dealt with in this essay.

There is a simple rule of thumb to tell entrepreneurs from non-entrepreneurs. The entrepreneurs are those on whom the incidence of losses on the capital employed falls. Amateur economists may confuse profits with other kinds of intakes. But it is impossible to fail to recognize losses on the capital employed.

3. Non-Profit Conduct of Affair

What has been called the democracy of the market manifests itself in the fact that profit-seeking business is unconditionally subject to the supremacy of the buying public.

Non-profit organizations are sovereign unto themselves. They are, within the limits drawn by the amount of capital at their disposal, in a position to defy the wishes of the public.

In the eyes of the laymen, the stockholders, promoters, and speculators, are merely idle parasites who pocket the dividends.

A special case is that of the conduct of government affairs, the administration of the social apparatus of coercion and oppression, viz. the police power. The objectives of government, the protection of the inviolability of the individuals' lives and health and of their efforts to improve the material conditions of their existence, are indispensable. They benefit all and are the necessary prerequisite of social cooperation and civilization. But they cannot be sold and bought in the way merchandise is sold and bought; they have therefore no price on the market. With regard to them there cannot be any economic calculation. The costs expended for their conduct cannot be confronted with a price received for the product. This state of affairs would make the officers entrusted with the administration of governmental activities irresponsible despots if they were not curbed by the budget system. Under this system the administrators are forced to comply with detailed instructions enjoined upon them by the sovereign, be it a self-appointed autocrat or the whole people acting through elected representatives. To the officers limited funds are assigned which they are bound to spend only for those purposes which the sovereign has ordered. Thus the management of public administration becomes bureaucratic, i.e., dependent on definite detailed rules and regulations.

Bureaucratic management is the only alternative available where there is no profit and loss management.[41]

4. The Ballot of the Market

The consumers by their buying and abstention from buying elect the entrepreneurs in a daily repeated plebiscite as it were. They determine who should own and who not, and how much each owner should own.

As is the case with all acts of choosing a person — choosing holders of public office, employees, friends, or a consort — the decision of the consumers is made on the ground of experience and thus necessarily always refers to the past. There is no experience of the future. The ballot of the market elevates those who in the immediate past have best served the consumers. However, the choice is not unalterable and can daily be corrected. The elected who disappoints the electorate is speedily reduced to the ranks.

Each ballot of the consumers adds only a little to the elected man's sphere of action. To reach the upper levels of entrepreneurship he needs a great number of votes, repeated again and again over a long period of time, a protracted series of successful strokes. He must stand every day a new trial, must submit anew to reelection as it were.

---

41 Cf. Mises, *Human Action*, Yale University Press, 1949, pages 305-07; *Bureaucracy*, Yale University Press, 1944, Pages 40-73.

It is the same with his heirs. They can retain their eminent position only by receiving again and again confirmation on the part of the public. Their office is revocable. If they retain it, it is not on account of the desserts of their predecessor, but on account of their own ability to employ the capital for the best possible satisfaction of the consumers.

The entrepreneurs are neither perfect nor good in any metaphysical sense. They owe their position exclusively to the fact that they are better fit for the performance of the functions incumbent upon them than other people are. They earn profit not because they are clever in performing their tasks, but because they are more clever or less clumsy than other people are. They are not infallible and often blunder. But they are less liable to error and blunder less than other people do. Nobody has the right to take offense at the errors made by the entrepreneurs in the conduct of affairs and to stress the point that people would have been better supplied if the entrepreneurs had been more skillful and prescient. If the grumbler knew better, why did he not himself fill the gap and seize the opportunity to earn profits? It is easy indeed to display foresight after the event. In retrospect all fools become wise.

A popular chain of reasoning runs this way: The entrepreneur earns profit not only on account of the fact that other people were less successful than he in anticipating correctly the future state of the market. He himself contributed to the emergence of profit by not producing more of the article concerned; but for intentional restriction of output on his part, the supply of this article would have been so ample that the price would have dropped to a point at which no surplus of proceeds over costs of production expended would have emerged. This reasoning is at the bottom of the spurious doctrines of imperfect and monopolistic competition. It was resorted to a short time ago by the American Administration when it blamed the enterprises of the steel industry for the fact that the steel production capacity of the United States was not greater than it really was.

Certainly those engaged in the production of steel are not responsible for the fact that other people did not likewise enter this field of production. The reproach on the part of the authorities would have been sensible if they had conferred on the existing steel corporations the monopoly of steel production. But in the absence of such a privilege, the reprimand given to the operating mills is not more justified than it would be to censure the nation's poets and musicians for the fact that there are not more and better poets and musicians. If somebody is to blame for the fact that the number of people who joined the voluntary civilian defense organization is not larger, then it is not those who have already joined but only those who have not.

That the production of a commodity *p* is not larger than it really is, is due to the fact that the complementary factors of production required for an expansion were employed for the production of other commodities. To speak of an insufficiency of the supply of *p* is empty rhetoric if it does not indicate the various products of which were produced in too large quantities with the effect that their production appears now, i.e., after the event, as a waste of scarce factors of production. We may assume that the entrepreneurs who instead of producing additional quantities of *p* turned to the production of excessive amounts of m and consequently suffered losses, did not intentionally make their mistake.

Neither did the producers of *p* intentionally restrict the production of p. Every entrepreneur's capital is limited; he employs it for those projects which, he expects, will, by filling the most urgent demand of the public, yield the highest profit.

An entrepreneur at whose disposal are 100 units of capital employs, for instance, 50 units for the production of *p* and 50 units for the production of q. If both lines are profitable, it is odd to blame him for not having employed more, e.g., 75 units, for the production of p. He could increase the production of *p* only by curtailing correspondingly the production of q. But with regard to *q* the same fault could be found by the grumblers. If one blames the entrepreneur for not having produced more p, one must blame him also for not having produced more q. This means: one blames the entrepreneur for the facts that there is a scarcity of the factors of production and that the earth is not a land of Cockaigne.

Perhaps the grumbler will object on the ground that he considers *p* a vital commodity, much more important than q, and that therefore the production of *p* should be expanded and that of *q* restricted. If this is really the meaning of his criticism, he is at variance with the valuations of the consumers. He throws off his mask and shows his dictatorial aspirations. Production should not be directed by the wishes of the public but by his own despotic discretion. But if our entrepreneur's production of *q* involves a loss, it is obvious that his fault was poor foresight and not intentional.

Entrance into the ranks of the entrepreneurs in a market society, not sabotaged by the interference of government or other agencies resorting to violence, is open to everybody. Those who know how to take advantage of any business opportunity cropping up will always find the capital required. For the market is always full of capitalists anxious to find the most promising employment for their funds and in search of the ingenious newcomers, in partnership with whom they could execute the most remunerative projects.

People often failed to realize this inherent feature of capitalism because they did not grasp the meaning and the effects of capital scarcity. The task of the entrepreneur is to select from the multitude of technologically feasible projects those which will satisfy the most urgent of the not yet satisfied needs of the public. Those projects for the execution of which the capital supply does not suffice must not be carried out. The market is always crammed with visionaries who want to float such impracticable and unworkable schemes. It is these dreamers who always complain about the blindness of the capitalists who are too stupid to look after their own interests. Of course, the investors often err in the choice of their investments. But these faults consist precisely in the fact that they preferred an unsuitable project to another that would have satisfied more urgent needs of the buying public.

People often err very lamentably in estimating the work of the creative genius. Only a minority of men are appreciative enough to attach the right value to the achievement of poets, artists, and thinkers. It may happen that the indifference of his contemporaries makes it impossible for a genius to accomplish what he would have accomplished if his fellow men had displayed better judgment. The way in which the poet laureate and the philosopher à la mode are selected is certainly questionable.

But it is impermissible to question the free market's choice of the entrepreneurs. The consumers' preference for definite articles may he open to condemnation from the point of view of a philosopher's judgment. But judgments of value are necessarily always personal and subjective. The consumer chooses what, as he thinks, satisfies him best. Nobody is called upon to determine what could make another man happier or less unhappy. The popularity of motor cars, television sets and nylon stockings may be criticized from a "higher" point of view. But these are the things that people are asking for. They cast their ballots for those entrepreneurs who offer them this merchandise of the best quality at the cheapest price.

In choosing between various political parties and programs for the commonwealth's social and economic organization most people are uninformed and groping in the dark. The average voter lacks the insight to distinguish between policies suitable to attain the ends he is aiming at and those unsuitable. He is at a loss to examine the long chains of aprioristic reasoning which constitute the philosophy of a comprehensive social program. He may at best form some opinion about the short-run effects of the policies concerned. He is helpless in dealing with the long-run effects. The socialists and communists in principle often assert the infallibility of majority decisions. However, they belie their own words in criticizing parliamentary majorities rejecting their creed, and in denying to the people, under the one-party system, the opportunity to choose between different parties.

But in buying a commodity or abstaining from its purchase there is nothing else involved than the consumer's longing for the best possible satisfaction of his instantaneous wishes. The consumer does not — like the voter in political voting — choose between different means whose effects appear only later. He chooses between things which immediately provide satisfaction. His decision is final.

An entrepreneur earns profit by serving the consumers, the people, as they are and not as they should be according to the fancies of some grumbler or potential dictator.

5. The Social Function of Profit and Loss

Profits are never normal. They appear only where there is a maladjustment, a divergence between actual production and production as it should be in order to utilize the available material and mental resources for the best possible satisfaction of the wishes of the public. They are the prize of those who remove this maladjustment; they disappear as soon as the maladjustment is entirely removed. In the imaginary construction of an evenly rotating economy there are no profits. There the sum of the prices of the complementary factors of production, due allowance being made for time preference, coincides with the price of the product.

The greater the preceding maladjustments, the greater the profit earned by their removal. Maladjustments may sometimes be called excessive. But it is inappropriate to apply the epithet "excessive" to profits.

People arrive at the idea of excessive profits by confronting the profit earned with the capital employed in the enterprise and measuring the profit as a percentage of the capital. This method is suggested by the customary procedure applied in partnerships and corporations for the assignment of quotas of the total profit to the individual partners and shareholders. These men have contributed to a different extent to the realization of the project and share in the profits and losses according to the extent of their contribution.

But it is not the capital employed that creates profits and losses. Capital does not "beget profit" as Marx thought. The capital goods as such are dead things that in themselves do not accomplish anything. If they are utilized according to a good idea, profit results. If they are utilized according to a mistaken idea, no profit or losses result. It is the entrepreneurial decision that creates either profit or loss. It is mental acts, the mind of the entrepreneur, from which profits ultimately originate. Profit is a product of the mind, of success in anticipating the future state of the market. It is a spiritual and intellectual phenomenon.

The absurdity of condemning any profits as excessive can easily be shown. An enterprise with a capital of the amount c produced a definite quantity of p which it sold at prices that brought a surplus of proceeds over costs of s and consequently a profit of n per cent. If the entrepreneur had been less capable, he would have needed a capital of 2c for the production of the same quantity of p. For the sake of argument we may even neglect the fact that this would have necessarily increased costs of production as it would have doubled the interest on the capital employed, and we may assume that s would have remained unchanged. But at any rate s would have been confronted with 2c instead of c and thus the profit would have been only n/2 percent of the capital employed. The "excessive" profit would have been reduced to a "fair" level. Why? Because the entrepreneur was less efficient and because his lack of efficiency deprived his fellow men of all the advantages they could have got if an amount c of capital goods had been left available for the production of other merchandise.

In branding profits as excessive and penalizing the efficient entrepreneurs by discriminatory taxation, people are injuring themselves. Taxing profits is tantamount to taxing success in best serving the public. The only goal of all production activities is to employ the factors of production in such a way that they render the highest possible output. The smaller the input required for the production of an article becomes, the more of the scarce factors of production is left for the production of other articles. But the better an entrepreneur succeeds in this regard, the more is he vilified and the more is he soaked by taxation. Increasing costs per unit of output, that is, waste, is praised as a virtue.

The most amazing manifestation of this complete failure to grasp the task of production and the nature and functions of profit and loss is shown in the popular superstition that profit is an addendum to the costs of production, the height of which depends uniquely on the discretion of the seller. It is this belief that guides governments in controlling prices. It is the same belief that has prompted many governments to make arrangements with their contractors according to which the price to be paid for an article delivered is to equal costs of production expended by the seller increased by a definite percentage. The effect was that the purveyor got a surplus the higher, the less he succeeded in avoiding superfluous costs.

Contracts of this type enhanced considerably the sums the United States had to expend in the two World Wars. But the bureaucrats, first of all the professors of economics who served in the various war agencies, boasted of their clever handling of the matter.

All people, entrepreneurs as well as non-entrepreneurs, look askance upon any profits earned by other people. Envy is a common weakness of men. People are loath to acknowledge the fact that they themselves could have earned profits if they had displayed the same foresight and judgment the successful businessman did. Their resentment is the more violent, the more they are subconsciously aware of this fact.

There would not be any profits but for the eagerness of the public to acquire the merchandise offered for sale by the successful entrepreneur. But the same people who scramble for these articles vilify the businessman and call his profit ill-got.

The semantic expression of this enviousness is the distinction between earned and unearned income. It permeates the textbooks, the language of the laws and administrative procedure. Thus, for instance, the official Form 201 for the New York State Income Tax Return calls "Earnings" only the compensation received by employees and, by implication, all other income, also that resulting from the exercise of a profession, unearned income. Such is the terminology of a state whose governor is a Republican and whose state assembly has a Republican majority.

Public opinion condones profits only as far as they do not exceed the salary paid to an employee. All surplus is rejected as unfair. The objective of taxation is, under the ability-to-pay principle, to confiscate this surplus.

Now one of the main functions of profits is to shift the control of capital to those who know how to employ it in the best possible way for the satisfaction of the public. The more profits a man earns, the greater his wealth consequently becomes, the more influential does he become in the conduct of business affairs. Profit and loss are the instruments by means of which the consumers pass the direction of production activities into the hands of those who are best fit to serve them. Whatever is undertaken to curtail or to confiscate profits impairs this function. The result of such measures is to loosen the grip the consumers hold over the course of production. The economic machine becomes, from the point of view of the people, less efficient and less responsive.

The jealousy of the common man looks upon the profits of the entrepreneurs as if they were totally used for consumption. A part of them is, of course, consumed. But only those entrepreneurs attain wealth and influence in the realm of business who consume merely a fraction of their proceeds and plough back the much greater part into their enterprises. What makes small business develop into big business is not spending, but saving and capital accumulation.

6. Profit and Loss in the Progressing and in the Retrogressing Economy

We call a stationary economy an economy in which the per head quota of the income and wealth of the individuals remains unchanged. In such an economy what the consumers spend more for the purchase of some articles must be equal to what they spend less for other articles. The total amount of the profits earned by one part of the entrepreneurs equals the total amount of losses suffered by other entrepreneurs.

"Profit is a product of the mind, of success in anticipating the future state of the market."

A surplus of the sum of all profits earned in the whole economy above the sum of all losses suffered emerges only in a progressing economy, that is in an economy in which the per head quota of capital increases. This increment is an effect of saving that adds new capital goods to the quantity already previously available. The increase of capital available creates maladjustments insofar as it brings about a discrepancy between the actual state of production and that state which the additional capital makes possible. Thanks to the emergence of additional capital, certain projects which hitherto could not be executed become feasible. In directing the new capital into those channels in which it satisfies the most urgent among the previously not satisfied wants of the consumers, the entrepreneurs earn profits which are not counterbalanced by the losses of other entrepreneurs.

The enrichment which the additional capital generates goes only in part to those who have created it by saving. The rest goes, by raising the marginal productivity of labor and thereby wage rates, to the earners of wages and salaries and, by raising the prices of definite raw materials and foodstuffs, to the owners of land, and, finally, to the entrepreneurs who integrate this new capital into the most economical production processes. But while the gain of the wage earners and of the landowners is permanent, the profits of the entrepreneurs disappear once this integration is accomplished. Profits of the entrepreneurs are, as has been mentioned already, a permanent phenomenon only on account of the fact that maladjustments appear daily anew by the elimination of which profits are earned.

Let us for the sake of argument resort to the concept of national income as employed in popular economics. Then it is obvious that in a stationary economy no part of the national income goes into profits. Only in a progressing economy is there a surplus of total profits over total losses. The popular belief that profits are a deduction from the income of workers and consumers is entirely fallacious. If we want to apply the term deduction to the issue, we have to say that this surplus of profits over losses as well as the increments of the wage earners and the landowners is deducted from the gains of those whose saving brought about the additional capital. It is their saving that is the vehicle of economic improvement, that makes the employment of technological innovations possible and raises productivity and the standard of living. It is the entrepreneurs whose activity takes care of the most economical employment of the additional capital. As far as they themselves do not save, neither the workers nor the landowners contribute anything to the emergence of the circumstances which generate what is called economic progress and improvement. They are benefited by other peoples' saving that creates additional capital on the one hand and by the entrepreneurial action that directs this additional capital toward the satisfaction of the most urgent wants on the other hand. A retrogressing economy is an economy in which the per head quota of capital invested is decreasing. In such an economy the total amount of losses incurred by entrepreneurs exceeds the total amount of profits earned by other entrepreneurs.

7. The Computation of Profit and Loss

The originary praxeological categories of profit and loss are psychic qualities and not reducible to any interpersonal description in quantitative terms. They are intensive magnitudes. The difference between the value of the end attained and that of the means applied for its attainment is profit if it is positive and loss if it is negative.

Where there are social division of efforts and cooperation as well as private ownership of the means of production, economic calculation in terms of monetary units becomes feasible and necessary. Profit and loss are computable as social phenomena. The psychic phenomena of profit and loss, from which they are ultimately derived, remain, of course, incalculable intensive magnitudes.

The fact that in the frame of the market economy entrepreneurial profit and loss are determined by arithmetical operations has misled many people. They fail to see that essential items that enter into this calculation are estimates emanating from the entrepreneur's specific understanding of the future state of the market. They think that these computations are open to examination and verification or alteration on the part of a disinterested expert. They ignore the fact that such computations are as a rule an inherent part of the entrepreneur's speculative anticipation of uncertain future conditions.

For the task of this essay it suffices to refer to one of the problems of cost accounting. One of the items of a bill of costs is the establishment of the difference between the price paid for the acquisition of what is commonly called durable production equipment and its present value. This present value is the money equivalent of the contribution this equipment will make to future earnings. There is no certainty about the future state of the market and about the height of these earnings. They can only be determined by a speculative anticipation on the part of the entrepreneur. It is preposterous to call in an expert and to substitute his arbitrary judgment for that of the entrepreneur. The expert is objective insofar as he is not affected by an error made. But the entrepreneur exposes his own material well-being.

Of course, the law determines magnitudes which it calls profit and loss. But these magnitudes are not identical with the economic concepts of profit and loss and must not be confused with them. If a tax law calls a magnitude profit, it in effect determines the height of taxes due. It calls this magnitude profit because it wants to justify its tax policy in the eyes of the public. It would be more correct for the legislator to omit the term profit and simply to speak of the basis for the computation of the tax due.

The tendency of the tax laws is to compute what they call profit as high as possible in order to increase immediate public revenue. But there are other laws which are committed to the tendency to restrict the magnitude they call profit. The commercial codes of many nations were and are guided by the endeavor to protect the rights of creditors. They aimed at restricting what they called profit in order to prevent the entrepreneur from withdrawing to the prejudice of creditors too much from the firm or corporation for his own benefit. It was these tendencies which were operative in the evolution of the commercial usages concerning the customary height of depreciation quotas.

There is no need today to dwell upon the problem of the falsification of economic calculation under inflationary conditions. All people begin to comprehend the phenomenon of illusory profits, the offshoot of the great inflations of our age.

Failure to grasp the effects of inflation upon the customary methods of computing profits originated the modern concept of *profiteering*. An entrepreneur is dubbed a profiteer if his profit and loss statement, calculated in terms of a currency subject to a rapidly progressing inflation, shows profits which other people deem "excessive." It has happened very often in many countries that the profit and loss statement of such a profiteer, when calculated in terms of a noninflated or less inflated currency, showed not only no profit at all but considerable losses.

Even if we neglect for the sake of argument any reference to the phenomenon of merely inflation-induced illusory profits, it is obvious that the epithet profiteer is the expression of an arbitrary judgment of value. There is no other standard available for the distinction between profiteering and earning fair profits than that provided by the censor's personal envy and resentment.

It is strange indeed that an eminent logician, the late L. Susan Stebbing, entirely failed to perceive the issue involved. Professor Stebbing equated the concept of profiteering to concepts which refer to a clear distinction of such a nature that no sharp line can be drawn between extremes. The distinction between excess profits or profiteering, and "legitimate profits," she declared, is clear, although it is not a sharp distinction.[42] Now this distinction is clear only in reference to an act of legislation that defines the term excess profits as used in its context. But this is not what Stebbing had in mind. She explicitly emphasized that such legal definitions are made "in an arbitrary manner for the practical purposes of administration." She used the term legitimate without any reference to legal statutes and their definitions. But is it

---

42 Cf. L. Susan Stebbing, *Thinking to Some Purpose*. (Pelican Books A44), pp. 185-187.

permissible to employ the term *legitimate* without reference to any standard from the point of view of which the thing in question is to be considered as legitimate? And is there any other standard available for the distinction between profiteering and legitimate profits than one provided by personal judgments of value?

Professor Stebbing referred to the famous *acervus* and *calvus* arguments of the old logicians. Many words are vague insofar as they apply to characteristics which may be possessed in varying degrees. It is impossible to draw a sharp line between those who are bald and those who are not. It is impossible to define precisely the concept of baldness. But what Professor Stebbing failed to notice is that the characteristic according to which people distinguish between those who are bald and those who are not is open to a precise definition. It is the presence or the absence of hair on the head of a person. This is a clear and unambiguous mark of which the presence or absence is to be established by observation and to be expressed by propositions about existence. What is vague is merely the determination of the point at which non-baldness turns into baldness. People may disagree with regard to the determination of this point. But their disagreement refers to the interpretation of the convention that attaches a certain meaning to the word baldness. No judgments of value are implied. It may, of course, happen that the difference of opinion is in a concrete case caused by bias. But this is another thing.

The vagueness of words like bald is the same that is inherent in the indefinite numerals and pronouns. Language needs such terms as for many purposes of daily communication between men an exact arithmetical establishment of quantities is superfluous and too bothersome. Logicians are badly mistaken in attempting to attach to such words whose vagueness is intentional and serves definite purposes the precision of the definite numerals. For an individual who plans to visit Seattle the information that there are many hotels in this city is sufficient. A committee that plans to hold a convention in Seattle needs precise information about the number of hotel beds available.

Professor Stebbing's error consisted in the confusion of existential propositions with judgments of value. Her unfamiliarity with the problems of economics, which all her otherwise valuable writings display, led her astray. She would not have made such a blunder in a field that was better known to her. She would not have declared that there is a clear distinction between an author's "legitimate royalties" and "illegitimate royalties." She would have comprehended that the height of the royalties depends on the public's appreciation of a book and that an observer who criticizes the height of royalties merely expresses his personal judgment of value.

B. The Condemnation of Profit

1. Economics and the Abolition of Profit

Those who spurn entrepreneurial profit as "unearned" mean that it is lucre unfairly withheld either from the workers or from the consumers or from both. Such is the idea underlying the alleged "right to the whole produce of labor" and the Marxian doctrine of exploitation. It can be said that most governments — if not all — and the immense majority of our contemporaries by and large endorse this opinion although some of them are generous enough to acquiesce in the suggestion that a fraction of profits should be left to the "exploiters."

There is no use in arguing about the adequacy of ethical precepts. They are derived from intuition; they are arbitrary and subjective. There is no objective standard available with regard to which they could be judged. Ultimate ends are chosen by the individual's judgments of value. They cannot be determined by scientific inquiry and logical reasoning. If a man says, "This is what I am aiming at whatever the consequences of my conduct and the price I shall have to pay for it may be," nobody is in a position to oppose any arguments against him. But the question is whether it is really true that this man is ready to pay any price for the attainment of the end concerned. If this latter question is answered in the negative, it becomes possible to enter into an examination of the issue involved.

If there were really people who are prepared to put up with all the consequences of the abolition of profit, however detrimental they may be, it would not be possible for economics to deal with the problem. But this is not the case. Those who want to abolish profit are guided by the idea that this confiscation would improve the material well-being of all non-entrepreneurs. In their eyes the abolition of profit is not an ultimate end but a means for the attainment of a definite end, viz., the enrichment of the non-entrepreneurs. Whether this end can really be attained by the employment of this means and whether the employment of this means does not perhaps bring about some other effects which may to some or to all people appear more undesirable than conditions before the employment of this means, these are questions which economics is called upon to examine.

2. The Consequences of the Abolition of Profit

The idea to abolish profit for the advantage of the consumers involves that the entrepreneur should be forced to sell the products at prices not exceeding the costs of production expended. As such prices are, for all articles the sale of which would have brought profit, below the potential market price, the available supply is not sufficient to make it possible for all those who want to buy at these prices to acquire the articles. The market is paralyzed by the maximum price decree. It can no longer allocate the products to the consumers. A system of rationing must be adopted.

The suggestion to abolish the entrepreneur's profit for the benefit of the employees aims not at the abolition of profit. It aims at wresting it from the hands of the entrepreneur and handing it over to his employees.

Under such a scheme the incidence of losses incurred falls

upon the entrepreneur, while profits go to the employees. It is probable that the effect of this arrangement would consist in making losses increase and profits dwindle. At any rate, a greater part of the profits would be consumed and less would be saved and ploughed back into the enterprise. No capital would be available for the establishment of new branches of production and for the transfer of capital from branches which — in compliance with the demand of the customers — should shrink into branches which should expand. For it would harm the interests of those employed in a definite enterprise or branch to restrict the capital employed in it and to transfer it into another enterprise or branch. If such a scheme had been adopted half a century ago, all the innovations accomplished in this period would have been rendered impossible. If, for the sake of argument, we were prepared to neglect any reference to the problem of capital accumulation, we would still have to realize that giving profit to the employees must result in rigidity of the once attained state of production and preclude any adjustment, improvement, and progress.

In fact, the scheme would transfer ownership of the capital invested into the hands of the employees. It would be tantamount to the establishment of syndicalism and would generate all the effects of syndicalism, a system which no author or reformer ever had the courage to advocate openly.

A third solution of the problem would be to confiscate all the profits earned by the entrepreneurs for the benefit of the state. A one hundred per cent tax on profits would accomplish this task. It would transform the entrepreneurs into irresponsible administrators of all plants and workshops. They would no longer be subject to the supremacy of the buying public. They would just be people who have the power to deal with production as it pleases them.

The policies of all contemporary governments which have not adopted outright socialism apply all these three schemes jointly. They confiscate by various measures of price control a part of the potential profits for the alleged benefit of the consumers. They support the labor unions in their endeavors to wrest, under the ability-to-pay principle of wage determination, a part of the profits from the entrepreneurs. And, last but not least, they are intent upon confiscating, by progressive income taxes, special taxes on corporation income and "excess profits" taxes, an ever increasing part of profits for public revenue. It can easily be seen that these policies if continued will very soon succeed in abolishing entrepreneurial profit altogether.

The joint effect of the application of these policies is already today rising chaos. The final effect will be the full realization of socialism by smoking out the entrepreneurs. Capitalism cannot survive the abolition of profit. It is profit and loss that force the capitalists to employ their capital for the best possible service to the consumers. It is profit and loss that make those people supreme in the conduct of business who are best fit to satisfy the public. If profit is abolished, chaos results.

3. The Anti-Profit Arguments

All the reasons advanced in favor of an anti-profit policy are the outcome of an erroneous interpretation of the operation of the market economy.

The tycoons are too powerful, too rich, and too big. They abuse their power for their own enrichment. They are irresponsible tyrants. Bigness of an enterprise is in itself an evil. There is no reason why some men should own millions while others are poor. The wealth of the few is the cause of the poverty of the masses.

Each word of these passionate denunciations is false. The businessmen are not irresponsible tyrants. It is precisely the necessity of making profits and avoiding losses that gives to the consumers a firm hold over the entrepreneurs and forces them to comply with the wishes of the people. What makes a firm big is its success in best filling the demands of the buyers. If the bigger enterprise did not better serve the people than a smaller one, it would long since have been reduced to smallness. There is no harm in a businessman's endeavors to enrich himself by increasing his profits. The businessman has in his capacity as a businessman only one task: to strive after the highest possible profit. Huge profits are the proof of good service rendered in supplying the consumers. Losses are the proof of blunders committed, of failure to perform satisfactorily the tasks incumbent upon an entrepreneur. The riches of successful entrepreneurs is not the cause of anybody's poverty; it is the consequence of the fact that the consumers are better supplied than they would have been in the absence of the entrepreneur's effort. The penury of millions in the backward countries is not caused by anybody's opulence; it is the correlative of the fact that their country lacks entrepreneurs who have acquired riches. The standard of living of the common man is highest in those countries which have the greatest number of wealthy entrepreneurs. It is to the foremost material interest of everybody that control of the factors of production should be concentrated in the hands of those who know how to utilize them in the most efficient way.

It is the avowed objective of the policies of all present-day governments and political parties to prevent the emergence of new millionaires. If this policy had been adopted in the United States fifty years ago, the, growth of the industries producing new articles would have been stunted. Motorcars, refrigerators, radio sets, and a hundred other less spectacular but even more useful innovations would not have become standard equipment of most of the American family households.

The average wage earner thinks that nothing else is needed to keep the social apparatus of production running and to improve and to increase output than the comparatively simple routine work assigned to him. He does not realize that the mere toil and trouble of the routinist is not sufficient. Sedulousness and skill are spent in vain if they are not directed toward the most important goal by the entrepreneur's foresight and are not aided by the capital accumulated by capitalists. The American worker is badly mistaken when he believes that his high standard of living is due to his own excellence. He is neither more industrious nor more skillful than the workers of Western Europe. He owes his superior income to the fact that his country clung to "rugged individualism" much longer than Europe. It was his luck that the United States turned to an anti-capitalistic policy as much as forty or fifty years later than Germany. His wages are higher than those of the workers of the rest of the world because the capital equipment per head of the employee is highest in America and because the American entrepreneur was not so much restricted by crippling regimentation as his colleagues in other areas. The comparatively greater prosperity of the United States is an outcome of the fact that the New Deal did not come in 1900 or 1910, but only in 1933.

If one wants to study the reasons for Europe's backwardness, it would be necessary to examine the manifold laws and regulations that prevented in Europe the establishment of an equivalent of the American drug store and crippled the evolution of chain stores, department stores, super markets, and kindred outfits. It would be important to investigate the German Reich's effort to protect the inefficient methods of traditional *Handwerk* (handicraft) against the competition of capitalist business. Still more revealing would be an examination of the Austrian *Gewerbepolitik*, a policy that from the early eighties on aimed at preserving the economic structure of the ages preceding the Industrial Revolution.

The worst menace to prosperity and civilization and to the material well-being of the wage earners is the inability of union bosses, of "union economists" and of the less intelligent strata of the workers themselves to appreciate the role entrepreneurs play in production. This lack of insight has found a classical expression in the writings of Lenin. As Lenin saw it all that production requires besides the manual work of the laborer and the designing of the engineers is "control of production and distribution," a task that can easily be accomplished "by the armed workers." For this accounting and control "have been *simplified* by capitalism to the utmost, till they have become the extraordinarily simple operations of watching, recording and issuing receipts, within the reach of everybody who can read and write and knows the first four rules of arithmetic."[43] No further comment is needed.

43 V.I. Lenin, *State and Revolution*, 1917 (Edition by International Publishers, New York, pages 83-84). The italics are Lenin's (or the communist translator's).

4. The Equality Argument

In the eyes of the parties who style themselves progressive and leftist the main vice of capitalism is the inequality of incomes and wealth. The ultimate end of their policies is to establish equality. The moderates want to attain this goal step by step; the radicals plan to attain it at one stroke, by a revolutionary overthrow of the capitalist mode of production.

However, in talking about equality and asking vehemently for its realization, nobody advocates a curtailment of his own present income. The term equality as employed in contemporary political language always means upward leveling of one's income, never downward leveling It means getting more, not sharing one's own affluence with people who have less.

If the American automobile worker, railroadman or compositor says equality, he means expropriating the holders of shares and bonds for his own benefit. He does not consider sharing with the unskilled workers who earn less. At best, he thinks of equality of all American citizens. It never occurs to him that the peoples of Latin America, Asia, and Africa may interpret the postulate of equality as world equality and not as national equality.

The political labor movement as well as the labor union movement flamboyantly advertise their internationalism. But this internationalism is a mere rhetorical gesture without any substantial meaning. In every country in which average wage rates are higher than in any other area, the unions advocate insurmountable immigration barriers in order to prevent foreign "comrades" and "brothers" from competing with their own members. Compared with the anti-immigration laws of the European nations, the immigration legislation of the American republics is mild indeed because it permits the immigration of a limited number of people. No such normal quotas are provided in most of the European laws.

"The standard of living of the common man is highest in those countries which have the greatest number of wealthy entrepreneurs."

All the arguments advanced in favor of income equalization within a country can with the same justification or lack of justification also be advanced in favor of world equalization. An American worker has no better title to claim the savings of the American capitalist than has any foreigner. That a man has earned profits by serving the consumers and has not entirely consumed his funds but ploughed back the greater part of them into industrial equipment does not give anybody a valid title to expropriate this capital for his own benefit. But if one maintains the opinion to the contrary, there is certainly no reason to ascribe to anybody a better right to expropriate than to anybody else. There is no reason to assert that only Americans have the right to expropriate other Americans. The big shots of American business are the scions of people who immigrated to the United States from England, Scotland, Ireland, France, Germany, and other European countries. The people of their country of origin contend that they have the same title to seize the property acquired by these men as the American people have. The American radicals are badly mistaken in believing that their social program is identical or at least compatible with the objectives of the radicals of other countries. It is not. The foreign radicals will not acquiesce in leaving to the Americans, a minority of less than 7% of the world's total population, what they think is a privileged position.

A world government of the kind the American radicals are asking for would try to confiscate by a world income tax all the surplus an average American earns above the average income of a Chinese or Indian worker. Those who question the correctness of this statement would drop their doubts after a conversation with any of the intellectual leaders of Asia.

There is hardly any Iranian who would qualify the objections raised by the British Labour Government against the confiscation of the oil wells as anything else but a manifestation of the most reactionary spirit of capitalist exploitation. Today governments abstain from virtually expropriating — by foreign exchange control, discriminatory taxation and similar devices — foreign investments only if they expect to get in the next years more foreign capital and thus to be able in the future to expropriate a greater amount.

The disintegration of the international capital market is one of the most important effects of the anti-profit mentality of our age. But no less disastrous is the fact that the greater part of the world's population looks upon the United States — not only upon the American capitalists but also upon the American workers — with the same feelings of envy, hatred, and hostility with which, stimulated by the socialist and communist doctrines, the masses everywhere look upon the capitalists of their own nation.

5. Communism and Poverty

A customary method of dealing with political programs and movements is to explain and to justify their popularity by referring to the conditions which people found unsatisfactory and to the goals they wanted to attain by the realization of these programs.

However, the only thing that matters is whether or not the program concerned is fit to attain the ends sought. A bad program and a bad policy can never be explained, still less justified by pointing to the unsatisfactory conditions of its originators and supporters. The sole question that counts is whether or not these policies can remove or alleviate the evils which they are designed to remedy.

Yet almost all our contemporaries declare again and again: If you want to succeed in fighting communism, socialism, and interventionism, you must first of all improve peoples' material conditions. The policy of laissez faire aims precisely at making people more prosperous. But it cannot succeed as long as want is worsened more and more by socialist and interventionist measures.

In the very short run the conditions of a part of the people can be improved by expropriating entrepreneurs and capitalists and by distributing the booty. But such predatory inroads, which even the Communist Manifesto described as "despotic" and as "economically insufficient and untenable," sabotage the operation of the market economy, impair very soon the conditions of all the people and frustrate the endeavors of entrepreneurs and capitalists to make the masses more prosperous. What is good for a quickly vanishing instant, (i.e., in the shortest run) may very soon (i.e., in the long run) result in most detrimental consequences.

Historians are mistaken in explaining the rise of Nazism by referring to real or imaginary adversities and hardships of the German people. What made the Germans support almost unanimously the twenty-five points of the "unalterable" Hitler program was not some conditions which they deemed unsatisfactory, but their expectation that the execution of this program would remove their complaints and render them happier. They turned to Nazism because they lacked common sense and intelligence. They were not judicious enough to recognize in time the disasters that Nazism was bound to bring upon them.

The immense majority of the world's population is extremely poor when compared with the average standard of living of the capitalist nations. But this poverty does not explain their propensity to adopt the communist program. They are anti-capitalistic because they are blinded by envy, ignorant, and too dull to appreciate correctly the causes of their distress. There is but one means to improve their material conditions, namely, to convince them that only capitalism can render them more prosperous.

The worst method to fight communism is that of the Marshall Plan. It gives to the recipients the impression that the United States alone is interested in the preservation of the profit system while their own concerns require a communist regime. The United States, they think, is aiding them because its people have a bad conscience. They themselves pocket this bribe but their sympathies go to the socialist system. The American subsidies make it possible for their governments to conceal partially the disastrous effects of the various socialist measures they have adopted.

Not poverty is the source of socialism, but spurious ideological prepossessions. Most of our contemporaries reject beforehand, without having ever studied them, all the teachings of economics as aprioristic nonsense. Only experience, they maintain, is to be relied upon. But is there any experience that would speak in favor of socialism?

Retorts the socialist: But capitalism creates poverty; look at India and China. The objection is vain. Neither India nor China has ever established capitalism. Their poverty is the result of the absence of capitalism.

What happened in these and other underdeveloped countries was that they were benefited from abroad by some of the fruits of capitalism without having adopted the capitalist mode of production. European, and in more recent years also American, capitalists invested capital in their areas and thereby increased the marginal productivity of labor and wage rates. At the same time these peoples received from abroad the means to fight contagious diseases, medications developed in the capitalist countries. Consequently mortality rates, especially infant mortality, dropped considerably. In the capitalist countries this prolongation of the average length of life was partially compensated by a drop in the birth rate. As capital accumulation increased more quickly than population, the per head quota of capital invested grew continuously. The result was progressing prosperity. It was different in the countries which enjoyed some of the effects of capitalism without turning to capitalism. There the birth rate did not decline at all or not to the extent required to make the per head quota of capital invested rise. These nations prevent by their policies both the importation of foreign capital and the accumulation of domestic capital. The joint effect of the high birth rate and the absence of an increase in capital is, of course, increasing poverty.

There is but one means to improve the material well-being of men, viz., to accelerate the increase in capital accumulated as against population. No psychological lucubrations, however sophisticated, can alter this fact. There is no excuse whatever for the pursuit of policies which not only fail to attain the ends sought, but even seriously impair conditions.

6. The Moral Condemnation of the Profit Motive

As soon as the problem of profits is raised, people shift it from the praxeological sphere into the sphere of ethical judgments of value. Then everybody glories in the aureole of a saint and an ascetic. He himself does not care for money and material well-being. He serves his fellow men to the best of his abilities unselfishly. He strives after higher and nobler things than wealth. Thank God, he is not one of those egoistic profiteers.

The businessmen are blamed because the only thing they have in mind is to succeed. Yet everybody — without any exception — in acting aims at the attainment of a definite end. The only alternative to success is failure; nobody ever wants to fail. It is the very essence of human nature that man consciously aims at substituting a more satisfactory state of affairs for a less satisfactory. What distinguishes the decent man from the crook is the different goals they are aiming at and the different means they are resorting to in order to attain the ends chosen. But they both want to succeed in their sense. It is logically impermissible to distinguish between people who aim at success and those who do not.

Practically everybody aims at improving the material conditions of his existence. Public opinion takes no offense at the endeavors of farmers, workers, clerks, teachers, doctors, ministers, and people from many other callings to earn as much as they can. But it censures the capitalists and entrepreneurs for their greed. While enjoying without any scruples all the goods business delivers, the consumer sharply condemns the selfishness of the purveyors of this merchandise. He does not realize that he himself creates their profits by scrambling for the things they have to sell.

Neither does the average man comprehend that profits are indispensable in order to direct the activities of business into those channels in which they serve him best. He looks upon profits as if their only function were to enable the recipients to consume more than he himself does. He fails to realize that their main function is to convey control of the factors of production into the hands of those who best utilize them for his own purposes. He did not, as he thinks, renounce becoming an entrepreneur out of moral scruples. He chose a position with a more modest yield because he lacked the abilities required for entrepreneurship or, in rare cases indeed, because his inclinations prompted him to enter upon another career.

Mankind ought to be grateful to those exceptional men who out of scientific zeal, humanitarian enthusiasm, or religious faith sacrificed their lives, health, and wealth, in the service of their fellow men. But the philistines practice self-deception in comparing themselves with the pioneers of medical X-ray application or with nuns who attend people afflicted with the plague. It is not self-denial that makes the average physician choose a medical career, but the expectation of attaining a respected social position and a suitable income.

Everybody is eager to charge for his services and accomplishments as much as the traffic can bear. In this regard there is no difference between the workers, whether unionized or not, the ministers, and teachers on the one hand and the entrepreneurs on the other hand. Neither of them has the right to talk as if he were Francis d'Assisi.

There is no other standard of what is morally good and morally bad than the effects produced by conduct upon social cooperation. A — hypothetical — isolated and self-sufficient individual would not in acting have to take into account anything else than his own well-being. Social man must in all his actions avoid indulging in any conduct that would jeopardize the smooth working of the system of social cooperation. In complying with the moral law, man does not sacrifice his own concerns to those of a mythical higher entity, whether it is called class, state, nation, race, or humanity. He curbs some of his own instinctive urges, appetites and greed, that is his short-run concerns, in order to serve best his own — rightly understood or long-run — interests. He foregoes a small gain that he could reap instantly lest he miss a greater but later satisfaction. For the attainment of all human ends, whatever they may be, is conditioned by the preservation and further development of social bonds and interhuman cooperation. What is an indispensable means to intensify social cooperation and to make it possible for more people to survive and to enjoy a higher standard of living is morally good and socially desirable. Those who reject this principle as unchristian ought to ponder over the text: "That thy days may be long upon the land which the Lord thy God giveth thee." They can certainly not deny that capitalism has made man's days longer than they were in the precapitalistic ages.

There is no reason why capitalists and entrepreneurs should

be ashamed of earning profits. It is silly that some people try to defend American capitalism by declaring: "The record of American business is good; profits are not too high." The function of entrepreneurs is to make profits; high profits are the proof that they have well performed their task of removing maladjustments of production.

Of course, as a rule capitalists and entrepreneurs are not saints excelling in the virtue of self-denial. But neither are their critics saintly. And with all the regard due to the sublime self-effacement of saints, we cannot help stating the fact that the world would be in a rather desolate condition if it were peopled exclusively by men not interested in the pursuit of material well-being.

7. The Static Mentality

The average man lacks the imagination to realize that the conditions of life and action are in a continual flux. As he sees it, there is no change in the external objects that constitute his well-being. His world view is static and stationary. It mirrors a stagnating environment. He knows neither that the past differed from the present nor that there prevails uncertainty about future things. He is at a complete loss to conceive the function of entrepreneurship because he is unaware of this uncertainty. Like children who take all the things the parents give them without asking any questions, he takes all the goods business offers him. He is unaware of the efforts that supply him with all he needs. He ignores the role of capital accumulation and of entrepreneurial decisions. He simply takes it for granted that a magic table appears at a moment's notice laden with all he wants to enjoy.

This mentality is reflected in the popular idea of socialization. Once the parasitic capitalists and entrepreneurs are thrown out, he himself will get all that they used to consume. It is but the minor error of this expectation that it grotesquely overrates the increment in income, if any, each individual could receive from such a distribution. Much more serious is the fact that it assumes that the only thing required is to continue in the various plants production of those goods they are producing at the moment of the socialization in the ways they were hitherto produced. No account is taken of the necessity to adjust production daily anew to perpetually changing conditions. The dilettante-socialist does not comprehend that a socialization effected fifty years ago would not have socialized the structure of business as it exists today but a very different structure. He does not give a thought to the enormous effort that is needed in order to transform business again and again to render the best possible service.

This dilettantish inability to comprehend the essential issues of the conduct of production affairs is not only manifested in the writings of Marx and Engels. It permeates no less the contributions of contemporary psuedo-economics.

The imaginary construction of an evenly rotating economy is an indispensable mental tool of economic thinking. In order to conceive the function of profit and loss, the economist constructs the image of a hypothetical, although unrealizable, state of affairs in which nothing changes, in which tomorrow does not differ at all from today and in which consequently no maladjustments can arise and no need for any alteration in the conduct of business emerges. In the frame of this imaginary construction there are no entrepreneurs and no entrepreneurial profits and losses. The wheels turn spontaneously as it were. But the real world in which men live and have to work can never duplicate the hypothetical world of this mental makeshift.

Now one of the main shortcomings of the mathematical economists is that they deal with this evenly rotating economy — they call it the static state — as if it were something really existing. Prepossessed by the fallacy that economics is to he treated with mathematical methods, they concentrate their efforts upon the analysis of static states which, of course, allow a description in sets of simultaneous differential equations. But this mathematical treatment virtually avoids any reference to the real problems of economics. It indulges in quite useless mathematical play without adding anything to the comprehension of the problems of human acting and producing. It creates the misunderstanding as if the analysis of static states were the main concern of economics. It confuses a merely ancillary tool of thinking with reality.

The mathematical economist is so blinded by his epistemological prejudice that he simply fails to see what the tasks of economics are. He is anxious to show us that socialism is realizable under static conditions. As static conditions, as he himself admits, are unrealizable, this amounts merely to the assertion that in an unrealizable state of the world socialism would be realizable. A very valuable result, indeed, of a hundred years of the joint work of hundreds of authors, taught at all universities, publicized in innumerable textbooks and monographs and in scores of allegedly scientific magazines!

There is no such thing as a static economy. All the conclusions derived from preoccupation with the image of static states and static equilibrium are of no avail for the description of the world as it is and will always be.

C. The Alternative

A social order based on private control of the means of production cannot work without entrepreneurial action and entrepreneurial profit and, of course, entrepreneurial loss. The elimination of profit, whatever methods may be resorted to for its execution, must transform society into a senseless jumble. It would create poverty for all.

In a socialist system there are neither entrepreneurs nor entrepreneurial profit and loss. The supreme director of the socialist commonwealth would, however, have to strive in the same way after a surplus of proceeds over costs as the entrepreneurs do under capitalism. It is not the task of this essay to deal with socialism. Therefore it is not necessary to stress the point that, not being able to apply any kind of economic calculation, the socialist chief would never know what the costs and what the proceeds of his operations are.

What matters in this context is merely the fact that there is no third system feasible. There cannot be any such thing as a non-socialist system without entrepreneurial profit and loss. The endeavors to eliminate profits from the capitalist system are merely destructive. They disintegrate capitalism without putting anything in its place. It is this that we have in mind in maintaining that they result in chaos.

Men must choose between capitalism and socialism. They cannot avoid this dilemma by resorting to a capitalist system without entrepreneurial profit. Every step toward the elimination of profit is progress on the way toward social disintegration.

In choosing between capitalism and socialism people are

implicitly also choosing between all the social institutions which are the necessary accompaniment of each of these systems, its "superstructure" as Marx said. If control of production is shifted from the hands of entrepreneurs, daily anew elected by a plebiscite of the consumers, into the hands of the supreme commander of the "industrial armies" (Marx and Engels) or of the "armed workers" (Lenin), neither representative government nor any civil liberties can survive. Wall Street, against which the self-styled idealists are battling, is merely a symbol. But the walls of the Soviet prisons within which all dissenters disappear forever are a hard fact.

ECONOMIC CALCULATION IN THE SOCIALIST COMMONWEALTH

This essay appeared in 1920 as "*Die Wirtschaftsrechnung im sozialistischen Gemeinwesen*" [Economic Calculation in the Socialist Commonwealth]. It was presented to the *Nation-alokonomische Gesellschaft*, later published in the *ArchivfUr Sozialwissenschaft und Sozialpolitik* (1920). etc.

Introduction by Ludwig von Mises (1920)

There are many socialists who have never come to grips in any way with the problems of economics, and who have made no attempt at all to form for themselves any clear conception of the conditions which determine the character of human society. There are others, who have probed deeply into the economic history of the past and present, and striven, on this basis, to construct a theory of economics of the "bourgeois" society. They have criticized freely enough the economic structure of "free" society, but have consistently neglected to apply to the economics of the disputed socialist state the same caustic acumen, which they have revealed elsewhere, not always with success. Economics, as such, figures all too sparsely in the glamorous pictures painted by the Utopians. They invariably explain how, in the cloud-cuckoo lands of their fancy, roast pigeons will in some way fly into the mouths of the comrades, but they omit to show how this miracle is to take place. Where they do in fact commence to be more explicit in the domain of economics, they soon find themselves at a loss—one remembers, for instance, Proudhon's fantastic dreams of an "exchange bank"—so that it is not difficult to point out their logical fallacies. When Marxism solemnly forbids its adherents to concern themselves with economic problems beyond the expropriation of the expropriators, it adopts no new principle, since the Utopians throughout their descriptions have also neglected all economic considerations, and concentrated attention solely upon painting lurid pictures of existing conditions and glowing pictures of that golden age which is the natural consequence of the New Dispensation.

Whether one regards the coming of socialism as an unavoidable result of human evolution, or considers the socialization of the means of production as the greatest blessing or the worst disaster that can befall mankind, one must at least concede, that investigation into the conditions of society organized upon a socialist basis is of value as something more than "a good mental exercise, and a means of promoting political clearness and consistency of thought."[44] In an age in which we are approaching nearer and nearer to socialism, and even, in a certain sense, are dominated by it, research into the problems of the socialist state acquires added significance for the explanation of what is going on around us. Previous analyses of the exchange economy no longer suffice for a proper understanding of social phenomena in Germany and its eastern neighbors today. Our task in this connection is to embrace within a fairly wide range the elements of socialistic society. Attempts to achieve clarity on this subject need no further justification.

1. The Distribution of Consumption Goods in the Socialist Commonwealth

Under socialism all the means of production are the property of the community. It is the community alone which can dispose of them and which determines their use in production. It goes without saying that the community will only be in a position to

44 Karl Kautsky, *The Social Revolution and On the Morrow of the Social Revolution* (London: Twentieth Century Press, 1907), Part II, p.1.

employ its powers of disposal through the setting up of a special body for the purpose. The structure of this body and the question of how it will articulate and represent the communal will is for us of subsidiary importance. One may assume that this last will depend upon the choice of personnel, and in cases where the power is not vested in a dictatorship, upon the majority vote of the members of the corporation.

The owner of production goods, who has manufactured consumption goods and thus becomes their owner, now has the choice of either consuming them himself or of having them consumed by others. But where the community becomes the owner of consumption goods, which it has acquired in production, such a choice will no longer obtain. It cannot itself consume; it has perforce to allow others to do so. Who is to do the consuming and what is to be consumed by each is the crux of the problem of socialist distribution.

It is characteristic of socialism that the distribution of consumption goods must be independent of the question of production and of its economic conditions. It is irreconcilable with the nature of the communal ownership of production goods that it should rely even for a part of its distribution upon the economic imputation of the yield to the particular factors of production. It is logically absurd to speak of the worker's enjoying the "full yield" of his work, and then to subject to a separate distribution the shares of the material factors of production. For, as we shall show, it lies in the very nature of socialist production that the shares of the particular factors of production in the national dividend cannot be ascertained, and that it is impossible in fact to gauge the relationship between expenditure and income.

What basis will be chosen for the distribution of consumption goods among the individual comrades is for us a consideration of more or less secondary importance. Whether they will be apportioned according to individual needs, so that he gets most who needs most, or whether the superior man is to receive more than the inferior, or whether a strictly equal distribution is envisaged as the ideal, or whether service to the State is to be the criterion, is immaterial to the fact that, in any event, the portions will be meted out by the State.

Let us assume the simple proposition that distribution will be determined upon the principle that the State treats all its members alike; it is not difficult to conceive of a number of peculiarities such as age, sex, health, occupation, etc., according to which what each receives will be graded. Each comrade receives a bundle of coupons, redeemable within a certain period against a definite quantity of certain specified goods. And so he can eat several times a day, find permanent lodgings, occasional amusements and a new suit every now and again. Whether such provision for these needs is ample or not, will depend on the productivity of social labor.

Moreover, it is not necessary that every man should consume the whole of his portion. He may let some of it perish without consuming it; he may give it away in presents; he many even in so far as the nature of the goods permit, hoard it for future use. He can, however, also exchange some of them. The beer tippler will gladly dispose of non-alcoholic drinks allotted to him, if he can get more beer in exchange, whilst the teetotaler will be ready to give up his portion of drink if he can get other goods for it. The art lover will be willing to dispose of his cinema tickets in order the more often to hear good music; the Philistine will be quite prepared to give up the tickets which admit him to art exhibitions in return for opportunities for pleasure he more readily understands. They will all welcome exchanges. But the material of these exchanges will always be consumption goods. Production goods in a socialist commonwealth are exclusively communal; they are an inalienable property of the community, and thus res extra commercium.

The principle of exchange can thus operate freely in a socialist state within the narrow limits permitted. It need not always develop in the form of direct exchanges. The same grounds which have always existed for the building-up of indirect exchange will continue in a socialist state, to place advantages in the way of those who indulge in it. It follows that the socialist state will thus also afford room for the use of a universal medium of exchange—that is, of money. Its role will be fundamentally the same in a socialist as in a competitive society; in both it serves as the universal medium of exchange. Yet the significance of money in a society where the means of production are State controlled will be different from that which attaches to it in one where they are privately owned. It will be, in fact, incomparably narrower, since the material available for exchange will be narrower, inasmuch as it will be confined to consumption goods. Moreover, just because no production good will ever become the object of exchange, it will be impossible to determine its monetary value. Money could never fill in a socialist state the role it fills in a competitive society in determining the value of production goods. Calculation in terms of money will here be impossible.

The relationships which result from this system of exchange

between comrades cannot be disregarded by those responsible for the administration and distribution of products. They must take these relationships as their basis, when they seek to distribute goods per head in accordance with their exchange value. If, for instance 1 cigar becomes equal to 5 cigarettes, it will be impossible for the administration to fix the arbitrary value of 1 cigar = 3 cigarettes as a basis for the equal distribution of cigars and cigarettes respectively. If the tobacco coupons are not to be redeemed uniformly for each individual, partly against cigars, partly against cigarettes, and if some receive only cigars and others only cigarettes, either because that is their wish or because the coupon office cannot do anything else at the moment, the market conditions of exchange would then have to be observed. Otherwise everybody getting cigarettes would suffer as against those getting cigars. For the man who gets one cigar can exchange it for five cigarettes, and he is only marked down with three cigarettes.

Variations in exchange relations in the dealings between comrades will therefore entail corresponding variations in the administrations' estimates of the representative character of the different consumption-goods. Every such variation shows that a gap has appeared between the particular needs of comrades and their satisfactions because in fact, some one commodity is more strongly desired than another.

The administration will indeed take pains to bear this point in mind also as regards production. Articles in greater demand will have to be produced in greater quantities while production of those which are less demanded will have to suffer a curtailment. Such control may be possible, but one thing it will not be free to do; it must not leave it to the individual comrade to ask the value of his tobacco ticket either in cigars or cigarettes at will. If the comrade were to have the right of choice, then it might well be that the demand for cigars and cigarettes would exceed the supply, or vice versa, that cigars or cigarettes pile up in the distributing offices because no one will take them.

If one adopts the standpoint of the labor theory of value, the problem freely admits of a simple solution. The comrade is then marked up for every hour's work put in, and this entitles him to receive the product of one hour's labor, less the amount deducted for meeting such obligations of the community as a whole as maintenance of the unfit, education, etc.

Taking the amount deducted for covering communal expenses as one half of the labor product, each worker who had worked a full hour would be entitled only to obtain such amount of the product as really answered to half an hour's work. Accordingly, anybody who is in a position to offer twice the labor time taken in manufacturing an article, could take it from the market and transfer to his own use or consumption . For the clarification of our problem it will be better to assume that the State does not in fact deduct anything from the workers towards meeting its obligations, but instead imposes an income tax on its working members. In that way every hour of work put in would carry with it the right of taking for oneself such amount of goods as entailed an hour's work.

Yet such a manner of regulating distribution would be unworkable, since labor is not a uniform and homogeneous quantity. Between various types of labor there is necessarily a qualitative difference, which leads to a different valuation according to the difference in the conditions of demand for and supply of their products. For instance, the supply of pictures cannot be increased ceteris paribus, without damage to the quality of the product. Yet one cannot allow the laborer who had put in an hour of the most simple type of labor to be entitled to the product of an hour's higher type of labor. Hence, it becomes utterly impossible in any socialist community to posit a connection between the significance to the community of any type of labor and the apportionment of the yield of the communal process of production. The remuneration of labor cannot but proceed upon an arbitrary basis; it cannot be based upon the economic valuation of the yield as in a competitive state of society, where the means of production are in private hands, since—as we have seen—any such valuation is impossible in a socialist community. Economic realities impose clear limits to the community's power of fixing the remuneration of labor on an arbitrary basis: in no circumstances can the sum expended on wages exceed the income for any length of time.

Within these limits it can do as it will. It can rule forthwith that all labor is to be reckoned of equal worth, so that every hour of work, whatever its quality, entails the same reward; it can equally well make a distinction in regard to the quality of work done. Yet in both cases it must reserve the power to control the particular distribution of the labor product. It will never be able to arrange that he who has put in an hour's labor shall also have the right to consume the product of an hour's labor, even leaving aside the question of differences in the quality of the labor and the products, and assuming moreover that it would be possible to gauge the amount of labor represented by any given article. For, over and above the actual labor, the production of all economic goods entails also the cost of materials. An article in which more raw material is used can never be reckoned of equal value with one in which less is used.

2. The Nature of Economic Calculation

Every man who, in the course of economic life, takes a choice between the satisfaction of one need as against another, eo ipso makes a judgment of value. Such judgments of value at once include only the very satisfaction of the need itself; and from this they reflect back upon the goods of a lower, and then further upon goods of a higher order.[45] As a rule, the man who knows his own mind is in a position to value goods of a lower order. Under simple conditions it is also possible for him without much ado to form some judgment of the significance to him of goods of a higher order. But where the state of affairs is more involved and their interconnections not so easily discernible, subtler means must be employed to accomplish a correct[46] valuation of the means of production. It would not be difficult for a farmer in economic isolation to come by a distinction between the expansion of pasture-farming and the development of activity in the hunting field. In such a case the processes of production involved are relatively short and the expense and income entailed can be

45 [By "lower order" Mises refers to those goods made for final consumption, and by "higher order" those used in production.]

46 Using that term, of course, in the sense only of the valuating subject, and not in an objective and universally applicable sense.

easily gauged. But it is quite a different matter when the choice lies between the utilization of a water-course for the manufacture of electricity or the extension of a coal mine or the drawing up of plans for the better employment of the energies latent in raw coal. Here the roundabout processes of production are many and each is very lengthy; here the conditions necessary for the success of the enterprises which are to be initiated are diverse, so that one cannot apply merely vague valuations, but requires rather more exact estimates and some judgment of the economic issues actually involved.

Valuation can only take place in terms of units, yet it is impossible that there should ever be a unit of subjective use value for goods. Marginal utility does not posit any unit of value, since it is obvious that the value of two units of a given stock is necessarily greater than, but less than double, the value of a single unit. Judgments of value do not measure; they merely establish grades and scales.[47] Even Robinson Crusoe, when he has to make a decision where no ready judgment of value appears and where he has to construct one upon the basis of a more or less exact estimate, cannot operate solely with subjective use value, but must take into consideration the intersubstitutability of goods on the basis of which he can then form his estimates. In such circumstances it will be impossible for him to refer all things back to one unit. Rather will he, so far as he can, refer all the elements which have to be taken into account in forming his estimate to those economic goods which can be apprehended by

47 Franz Cuhel, Zur Lehre von den Bedürfnissen (Innsbruck: Wagner'ssche Universitüt-Buchhandlung, 1907), pp.198 f.

an obvious judgment of value < —that is to say, to goods of a lower order and to pain-cost. That this is only possible in very simple conditions is obvious. In the case of more complicated and more lengthy processes of production it will, plainly, not answer.

In an exchange economy the objective exchange value of commodities enters as the unit of economic calculation. This entails a threefold advantage. In the first place, it renders it possible to base the calculation upon the valuations of all participants in trade. The subjective use value of each is not immediately comparable as a purely individual phenomenon with the subjective use value of other men. It only becomes so in exchange value, which arises out of the interplay of the subjective valuations of all who take part in exchange. But in that case calculation by exchange value furnishes a control over the appropriate employment of goods. Anyone who wishes to make calculations in regard to a complicated process of production will immediately notice whether he has worked more economically than others or not; if he finds, from reference to the exchange relations obtaining in the market, that he will not be able to produce profitably, this shows that others understand how to make a better use of the goods of higher order in question. Lastly, calculation by exchange value makes it possible to refer values back to a unit. For this purpose, since goods are mutually substitutable in accordance with the exchange relations obtaining in the market, any possible good can be chosen. In a monetary economy it is money that is so chosen.

Monetary calculation has its limits. Money is no yardstick of value, nor yet of price. Value is not indeed measured in money, nor is price. They merely consist in money. Money as an economic good is not of stable value as has been naively, but wrongly, assumed in using it as a "standard of deferred payments." The exchange-relationship which obtains between money and goods is subjected to constant, if (as a rule) not too violent, fluctuations originating not only from the side of other economic goods, but also from the side of money. However, these fluctuations disturb value calculations only in the slightest degree, since usually, in view of the ceaseless alternations in other economic data—these calculations will refer only to comparatively short periods of time—periods in which "good" money, at least normally, undergoes comparatively trivial fluctuations in regard to its exchange relations. The inadequacy of the monetary calculation of value does not have its mainspring in the fact that value is then calculated in terms of a universal medium of exchange, namely money, but rather in the fact that in this system it is exchange value and not subjective use value on which the calculation is based. It can never obtain as a measure for the calculation of those value determining elements which stand outside the domain of exchange transactions. If, for example, a man were to calculate the profitability of erecting a waterworks, he would not be able to include in his calculation the beauty of the waterfall which the scheme might impair, except that he may pay attention to the diminution of tourist traffic or similar changes, which may be valued in terms of money. Yet these considerations might well prove one of the factors in deciding whether or not the building is to go up at all.

It is customary to term such elements "extra-economic. " This perhaps is appropriate; we are not concerned with disputes over terminology; yet the considerations themselves can scarcely be termed irrational. In any place where men regard as significant the beauty of a neighborhood or of a building, the health, happiness and contentment of mankind, the honor of individuals or nations, they are just as much motive forces of rational conduct as are economic factors in the proper sense of the word, even where they are not substitutable against each other on the market and therefore do not enter into exchange relationships.

That monetary calculation cannot embrace these factors lies in its very nature; but for the purposes of our everyday economic life this does not detract from the significance of monetary calculation. For all those ideal goods are goods of a lower order, and can hence be embraced straightway within the ambit of our judgment of values. There is therefore no difficulty in taking them into account, even though they must remain outside the sphere of monetary value. That they do not admit of such computation renders their consideration in the affairs of life easier and not harder. Once we see clearly how highly we value beauty, health, honor and pride, surely nothing can prevent us from paying a corresponding regard to them. It may seem painful to any sensitive spirit to have to balance spiritual goods against material. But that is not the fault of monetary calculation; it lies in the very nature of things themselves. Even where judgments of value can be established directly without computation in value or in money, the necessity of choosing between material and spiritual satisfaction cannot be evaded. Robinson Crusoe and the socialist state have an equal obligation to make the choice.

Anyone with a genuine sense of moral values experiences no hardship in deciding between honor and livelihood. He knows his plain duty. If a man cannot make honor his bread, yet can he renounce his bread for honor's sake. Only they who prefer to be relieved of the agony of this decision, because they cannot bring themselves to renounce material comfort for the sake of spiritual advantage, see in the choice a profanation of true values.

Monetary calculation only has meaning within the sphere of economic organization. It is a system whereby the rules of economics may be applied in the disposition of economic goods. Economic goods only have part in this system in proportion to the extent to which they may be exchanged for money. Any extension of the sphere of monetary calculation causes misunderstanding. It cannot be regarded as constituting a kind of yardstick for the valuation of goods, and cannot be so treated in historical investigations into the development of social relationships; it cannot be used as a criterion of national wealth and income, nor as a means of gauging the value of goods which stand outside the sphere of exchange, as who should seek to estimate the extent of human losses through emigrations or wars in terms of money?[48] This is mere sciolistic tomfoolery, however much it may be indulged in by otherwise perspicacious economists.

Nevertheless within these limits, which in economic life it never oversteps, monetary calculation fulfils all the requirements of economic calculation. It affords us a guide through the oppressive plenitude of economic potentialities. It enables us to extend to all goods of a higher order the judgment of value, which is bound up with and clearly evident in, the case of goods ready for consumption, or at best of production goods of the lowest

48 Cf. Friedrich von Wieser, *Über den Ursprung und die Hauptgesetze des wirtschaftlichen Eertes* (Vienna: A. Hölder, 1884), pp. 185 f.

order. It renders their value capable of computation and thereby gives us the primary basis for all economic operations with goods of a higher order. Without it, all production involving processes stretching well back in time and all the longer roundabout processes of capitalist production would be gropings in the dark.

There are two conditions governing the possibility of calculating value in terms of money. Firstly, not only must goods of a lower, but also those of a higher order, come within the ambit of exchange, if they are to be included. If they do not do so, exchange relationships would not arise. True enough, the considerations which must obtain in the case of Robinson Crusoe prepared, within the range of his own hearth, to exchange, by production, labor and flour for bread, are indistinguishable from those which obtain when he is prepared to exchange bread for clothes in the open market, and, therefore, it is to some extent true to say that every economic action, including Robinson Crusoe's own production, can be termed exchange.[49] Moreover, the mind of one man alone—be it ever so cunning, is too weak to grasp the importance of any single one among the countlessly many goods of a higher order. No single man can ever master all the possibilities of production, innumerable as they are, as to be in a position to make straightway evident judgments of value without the aid of some system of computation. The distribution among a number of individuals of administrative control over economic

---

49 Cf. Mises, *Theorie des Geldes und der Umlaufsmittel* (Munich and Leipzig: Duncker & Humblot, 1912), p. 16, with the references there given. [See the English translation by H.E. Batson, *The Theory of Money and Credit* (Indianapolis: Liberty Classics, 1980), p. 52.]

goods in a community of men who take part in the labor of producing them, and who are economically interested in them, entails a kind of intellectual division of labor, which would not be possible without some system of calculating production and without economy.

The second condition is that there exists in fact a universally employed medium of exchange—namely, money —which plays the same part as a medium in the exchange of production goods also. If this were not the case, it would not be possible to reduce all exchange-relationships to a common denominator.

Only under simple conditions can economics dispense with monetary calculation. Within the narrow confines of household economy, for instance, where the father can supervise the entire economic management, it is possible to determine the significance of changes in the processes of production, without such aids to the mind, and yet with more or less of accuracy. In such a case the process develops under a relatively limited use of capital. Few of the capitalistic roundabout processes of production are here introduced: what is manufactured is, as a rule, consumption goods or at least such goods of a higher order as stand very near to consumption-goods. The division of labor is in its rudimentary stages: one and the same laborer controls the labor of what is in effect, a complete process of production of goods ready for consumption, from beginning to end. All this is different, however, in developed communal production. The experiences of a remote and bygone period of simple production do not provide any sort of argument for establishing the possibility of an economic system without monetary calculation.

In the narrow confines of a closed household economy, it is

possible throughout to review the process of production from beginning to end, and to judge all the time whether one or another mode of procedure yields more consumable goods. This, however, is no longer possible in the incomparably more involved circumstances of our own social economy. It will be evident, even in the socialist society, that 1,000 hectolitres of wine are better than 800, and it is not difficult to decide whether it desires 1,000 hectolitres of wine rather than 500 of oil. There is no need for any system of calculation to establish this fact: the deciding element is the will of the economic subjects involved. But once this decision has been taken, the real task of rational economic direction only commences, i.e. economically, to place the means at the service of the end. That can only be done with some kind of economic calculation. The human mind cannot orientate itself properly among the bewildering mass of intermediate products and potentialities of production without such aid. It would simply stand perplexed before the problems of management and location.[50]

It is an illusion to imagine that in a socialist state calculation in natura can take the place of monetary calculation. Calculation in natura, in an economy without exchange, can embrace consumption goods only; it completely fails when it comes to dealing with goods of a higher order. And as soon as one gives up the conception of a freely established monetary price for goods of a higher order, rational production becomes completely impossible. Every step that takes us away from private ownership

---

50 Friedrich von Gottl-Ottlilienfeld, *Wirtschaft und technik* (Grundriss der Sozialökonomik, Section II; Tübingen: J.C.B. Mohr, 1914), p. 216.

of the means of production and from the use of money also takes us away from rational economics.

It is easy to overlook this fact, considering that the extent to which socialism is in evidence among us constitutes only a socialistic oasis in a society with monetary exchange, which is still a free society to a certain degree. In one sense we may agree with the socialists' assertion which is otherwise entirely untenable and advanced only as a demagogic point, to the effect that the nationalization and municipalization of enterprise is not really socialism, since these concerns in their business organizations are so much dependent upon the environing economic system with its free commerce that they cannot be said to partake today of the really essential nature of a socialist economy. In state and municipal undertakings technical improvements are introduced because their effect in similar private enterprises, domestic or foreign, can be noticed, and because those private industries which produce the materials for these improvements give the impulse for their introduction. In these concerns the advantages of reorganization can be established, because they operate within the sphere of a society based upon private ownership of the means of production and upon the system of monetary exchange, being thus capable of computation and account. This state of affairs, however, could not obtain in the case of socialist concerns operating in a purely socialistic environment.

Without economic calculation there can be no economy . Hence, in a socialist state wherein the pursuit of economic calculation is impossible, there can be—in our sense of the term—no economy whatsoever. In trivial and secondary matters rational conduct might still be possible, but in general it would be impossible to speak of rational production any more. There would be no means of determining what was rational, and hence it is obvious that production could never be directed by economic considerations. What this means is clear enough, apart from its effects on the supply of commodities. Rational conduct would be divorced from the very ground which is its proper domain. Would there, in fact, be any such thing as rational conduct at all, or, indeed, such a thing as rationality and logic in thought itself? Historically, human rationality is a development of economic life. Could it then obtain when divorced therefrom?

For a time the remembrance of the experiences gained in a competitive economy, which has obtained for some thousands of years, may provide a check to the complete collapse of the art of economy. The older methods of procedure might be retained not because of their rationality but because they appear to be hallowed by tradition. Actually, they would meanwhile have become irrational, as no longer comporting with the new conditions. Eventually, through the general reconstruction of economic thought, they will experience alterations which will render them in fact uneconomic. The supply of goods will no longer proceed anarchically of its own accord; that is true. All transactions which serve the purpose of meeting requirements will be subject to the control of a supreme authority. Yet in place of the economy of the "anarchic" method of production, recourse will be had to the senseless output of an absurd apparatus. The wheels will turn, but will run to no effect.

One may anticipate the nature of the future socialist society. There will be hundreds and thousands of factories in operation. Very few of these will be producing wares ready for use; in the majority of cases what will be manufactured will be unfinished goods and production goods. All these concerns will be interrelated. Every good will go through a whole series of stages before it is ready for use. In the ceaseless toil and moil of this process, however, the administration will be without any means of testing their bearings. It will never be able to determine whether a given good has not been kept for a superfluous length of time in the necessary processes of production, or whether work and material have not been wasted in its completion. How will it be able to decide whether this or that method of production is the more profitable? At best it will only be able to compare the quality and quantity of the consumable end product produced, but will in the rarest cases be in a position to compare the expenses entailed in production. It will know, or think it knows, the ends to be achieved by economic organization, and will have to regulate its activities accordingly, i.e. it will have to attain those ends with the least expense. It will have to make its computations with a view to finding the cheapest way. This computation will naturally have to be a value computation. It is eminently clear, and requires no further proof, that it cannot be of a technical character, and that it cannot be based upon the objective use value of goods and services.

Now, in the economic system of private ownership of the means of production, the system of computation by value is necessarily employed by each independent member of society. Everybody participates in its emergence in a double way: on the one hand as a consumer and on the other as a producer. As a consumer he establishes a scale of valuation for goods ready for use in consumption. As a producer he puts goods of a higher order into such use as produces the greatest return. In this way all goods of a higher order receive a position in the scale of valuations in accordance with the immediate state of social conditions of production and of social needs. Through the interplay of these two processes of valuation, means will be afforded for governing both consumption and production by the economic principle throughout. Every graded system of pricing proceeds from the fact that men always and ever harmonized their own requirements with their estimation of economic facts.

All this is necessarily absent from a socialist state. The administration may know exactly what goods are most urgently needed. But in so doing, it has only found what is, in fact, but one of the two necessary prerequisites for economic calculation. In the nature of the case it must, however, dispense with the other—the valuation of the means of production. It may establish the value attained by the totality of the means of production; this is obviously identical with that of all the needs thereby satisfied. It may also be able to calculate the value of any means of production by calculating the consequence of its withdrawal in relation to the satisfaction of needs. Yet it cannot reduce this value to the uniform expression of a money price, as can a competitive economy, wherein all prices can be referred back to a common expression in terms of money. In a socialist commonwealth which, whilst it need not of necessity dispense with money altogether, yet finds it impossible to use money as an expression of the price of the factors of production (including labor), money can play no role in economic calculation.[51]

Picture the building of a new railroad. Should it be built at all, and if so, which out of a number of conceivable roads should be built? In a competitive and monetary economy, this question would be answered by monetary calculation. The new road will render less expensive the transport of some goods, and it may be possible to calculate whether this reduction of expense transcends that involved in the building and upkeep of the next line. That can only be calculated in money. It is not possible to attain the desired end merely by counterbalancing the various physical expenses and physical savings. Where one cannot express hours of labor, iron, coal, all kinds of building material, machines and other things necessary for the construction and upkeep of the railroad in a common unit it is not possible to make calculations at all. The drawing up of bills on an economic basis is only possible where all the goods concerned can be referred back to money. Admittedly, monetary calculation has its inconveniences and serious defects, but we have certainly nothing better to put in its place, and for the practical purposes of life monetary calculation as it exists under a sound monetary system always suffices. Were we to dispense with it, any economic system of calculation would

---

51 This fact is also recognized by Otto Neurath (*Durch die Kriegswirtschaft zur Naturalwirtschaft* [Munich: G.D.W. Callwey, 1919], pp. 216 f.). He advances the view that every complete administrative economy is, in the final analysis, a natural economy. "Socialization," he says, "is thus the pursuit of natural economy." Neurath merely overlooks the insuperable difficulties that would have to develop with economic calculation in the socialist commonwealth.

become absolutely impossible.

The socialist society would know how to look after itself. It would issue an edict and decide for or against the projected building. Yet this decision would depend at best upon vague estimates; it would never be based upon the foundation of an exact calculation of value.

The static state can dispense with economic calculation. For here the same events in economic life are ever recurring; and if we assume that the first disposition of the static socialist economy follows on the basis of the final state of the competitive economy, we might at all events conceive of a socialist production system which is rationally controlled from an economic point of view. But this is only conceptually possible. For the moment, we leave aside the fact that a static state is impossible in real life, as our economic data are forever changing, so that the static nature of economic activity is only a theoretical assumption corresponding to no real state of affairs, however necessary it may be for our thinking and for the perfection of our knowledge of economics. Even so, we must assume that the transition to socialism must, as a consequence of the levelling out of the differences in income and the resultant readjustments in consumption, and therefore production, change all economic data in such a way that a connecting link with the final state of affairs in the previously existing competitive economy becomes impossible. But then we have the spectacle of a socialist economic order floundering in the ocean of possible and conceivable economic combinations without the compass of economic calculation.

Thus in the socialist commonwealth every economic change becomes an undertaking whose success can be neither appraised in advance nor later retrospectively determined. There is only groping in the dark. Socialism is the abolition of rational economy.

3. Economic Calculation in the Socialist Commonwealth

Are we really dealing with the necessary consequences of common ownership of the means of production? Is there no way in which some kind of economic calculation might be tied up with a socialist system?

In every great enterprise, each particular business or branch of business is to some extent independent in its accounting. It reckons the labor and material against each other, and it is always possible for each individual group to strike a particular balance and to approach the economic results of its activities from an accounting point of view. We can thus ascertain with what success each particular section has labored, and accordingly draw conclusions about the reorganization, curtailment, abandonment, or expansion of existing groups and about the institution of new ones. Admittedly, some mistakes are inevitable in such a calculation. They arise partly from the difficulties consequent upon an allocation of general expenses. Yet other mistakes arise from the necessity of calculating with what are not from many points of view rigorously ascertainable data, e.g. when in the ascertainment of the profitability of a certain method of procedure we compute the amortization of the machines used on the assumption of a given duration for their usefulness. Still, all such mistakes can be confined within certain narrow limits, so that they do not disturb the net result of the calculation. What remains of uncertainty comes into the calculation of the uncertainty of future conditions, which is an inevitable concomitant of the dynamic nature of economic life.

It seems tempting to try to construct by analogy a separate estimation of the particular production groups in the socialist state also. But it is quite impossible. For each separate calculation of the particular branches of one and the same enterprise depends exclusively on the fact that is precisely in market dealings that market prices to be taken as the bases of calculation are formed for all kinds of goods and labor employed. Where there is no free market, there is no pricing mechanism; without a pricing mechanism, there is no economic calculation.

We might conceive of a situation, in which exchange between particular branches of business is permitted, so as to obtain the mechanism of exchange relations (prices) and thus create a basis for economic calculation even in the socialist commonwealth. Within the framework of a uniform economy knowing not private ownership of the means of production, individual labor groups are constituted independent and authoritative disposers, which have indeed to behave in accordance with the directions of the supreme economic council, but which nevertheless assign each other material goods and services only against a payment, which would have to be made in the general medium of exchange. It is roughly in this way that we conceive of the organization of the socialist running of business when we nowadays talk of complete socialization and the like. But we have still not come to the crucial point. Exchange relations between production goods can only be established on the basis of private ownership of the means of production. When the "coal syndicate " provides the "iron syndicate " with coal, no price can be formed, except when both syndicates are the owners of the means of production employed in their business. This would not be socialization but workers' capitalism and syndicalism.

The matter is indeed very simple for those socialist theorists who rely on the labor theory of value.

> As soon as society takes possession of the means of production and applies them to production in their directly socialised form, each individual's labour, however different its specific utility may be, becomes a priori and directly social labour. The amount of social labour invested in a product need not then be established indirectly; daily experience immediately tells us how much is necessary on an average. Society can simply calculate how many hours of labour are invested in a steam engine, a quarter of last harvest's wheat, and a 100 yards of linen of given quality ... To be sure, society will also have to know how much labour is needed to produce any consumption-good. It will have to arrange its production plan according to its means of production, to which labour especially belongs. The utility yielded by the various consumption-goods, weighted against each other and against the amount of labour required to produce them, will ultimately determine the plan. People will make everything simple without the mediation of the notorious "value." [52]

52 Friedrich Engels, *Herrn Eugen Dührings Umwälzung des Wissenschaft*, 7th ed., pp. 335 f. [Translated by Emile Burns as *Herr Eugen Dühring's Revolution in Science—Anti-Dühring* (London: Lawrence & Wishart, 1943).]

Here it is not our task once more to advance critical objections against the labor theory of value. In this connection they can only interest us in so far as they are relevant to an assessment of the applicability of labor in the value computations of a socialist community.

On a first impression calculation in terms of labor also takes into consideration the natural non-human conditions of production. The law of diminishing returns is already allowed for in the concept of socially necessary average labor time to the extent that its operation is due to the variety of the natural conditions of production. If the demand for a commodity increases and worse natural resources must be exploited, then the average socially necessary labor time required for the production of a unit increases too. If more favorable natural resources are discovered, the amount of socially necessary labor diminishes.[53] The consideration of the natural condition of production suffices only in so far as it is reflected in the amount of labor socially necessary. But it is in this respect that valuation in terms of labor fails. It leaves the employment of material factors of production out of account. Let the amount of socially necessary labor time required for the production of each of the commodities P and Q be 10 hours. Further, in addition to labor the production of both P and Q requires the raw material a, a unit of which is produced by an hour's socially necessary labor; 2 units of a and 8 hours' labor are used in the production of P, and one unit of a and 9 hours' labor in the production of Q. In terms of labor P and Q are equivalent,

53 Karl Marx, *Capital*, translated by Eden and Cedar Paul (London: Allen & Unwin, 1928), p. 9.

but in value terms P is more valuable than Q. The former is false, and only the latter corresponds to the nature and purpose of calculation. True, this surplus, by which according to value calculation P is more valuable than Q, this material sub-stratum "is given by nature without any addition from man."[54] Still, the fact that it is only present in such quantities that it becomes an object of economizing, must be taken into account in some form or other in value calculation.

The second defect in calculation in terms of labor is the ignoring of the different qualities of labor. To Marx all human labor is economically of the same kind, as it is always "the productive expenditure of human brain, brawn, nerve and hand."[55]

> Skilled labour counts only as intensified, or rather multiplied, simple labour, so that a smaller quantity of skilled labour is equal to a larger quantity of simple labour. Experience shows that skilled labour can always be reduced in this way to the terms of simple labour. No matter that a commodity be the product of the most highly skilled labour, its value can be equated with that of the product of simple labour, so that it represents merely a definite amount of simple labour.

Böhm-Bawerk is not far wrong when he calls this argument

54 Karl Marx, *Capital*, translated by Eden and Cedar Paul (London: Allen & Unwin, 1928), p. 12.

55 Karl Marx, *Capital*, translated by Eden and Cedar Paul (London: Allen & Unwin, 1928), p. 13 et seq.

"a theoretical juggle of almost stupefying naïveté."[56] To judge Marx's view we need not ask if it is possible to discover a single uniform physiological measure of all human labor, whether it be physical or "mental." For it is certain that there exist among men varying degrees of capacity and dexterity, which cause the products and services of labor to have varying qualities. What must be conclusive in deciding the question whether reckoning in terms of labor is applicable or not, is whether it is or is not possible to bring different kinds of labor under a common denominator without the mediation of the economic subject's valuation of their products. The proof Marx attempts to give is not successful. Experience indeed shows that goods are consumed under exchange relations without regard of the fact of their being produced by simple or complex labor. But this would only be a proof that given amounts of simple labor are directly made equal to given amounts of complex labor, if it were shown that labor is their source of exchange value. This not only is not demonstrated, but is what Marx is trying to demonstrate by means of these very arguments.

No more is it a proof of this homogeneity that rates of substitution between simple and complex labor are manifested in the wage rate in an exchange economy—a fact to which Marx does not allude in this context. This equalizing process is a result of market transactions and not its antecedent. Calculation in terms of labor would have to set up an arbitrary proportion for the substitution of complex by simple labor, which excludes its

56 Cf. Eugen von Böhm-Bawerk, *Capital and Interest*, translated by William Smart (London and New York: Macmillan, 1890), p. 384.

employment for purposes of economic administration.

It was long supposed that the labor theory of value was indispensable to socialism, so that the demand for the nationalization of the means of production should have an ethical basis. Today we know this for the error it is. Although the majority of socialist supporters have thus employed this misconception, and although Marx, however much he fundamentally took another point of view, was not altogether free from it, it is clear that the political call for the introduction of socialized production neither requires nor can obtain the support of the labor theory of value on the one hand, and that on the other those people holding different views on the nature and origin of economic value can be socialist according to their sentiments. Yet the labor theory of value is inherently necessary for the supporters of socialist production in a sense other than that usually intended. In the main socialist production might only appear rationally realizable, if it provided an objectively recognizable unit of value, which would permit of economic calculation in an economy where neither money nor exchange were present. And only labor can conceivably be considered as such.

4. Responsibility and Initiative in Communal Concerns

The problem of responsibility and initiative in socialist enterprises is closely connected with that of economic calculation. It is now universally agreed that the exclusion of free initiative and individual responsibility, on which the successes of private enterprise depend, constitutes the most serious menace to socialist economic organization.[57]

The majority of socialists silently pass this problem by. Others believe they can answer it with an allusion to the directors of companies; in spite of the fact that they are not the owners of the means of production, enterprises under their control have flourished. If society, instead of company shareholders, becomes the owner of the means of production, nothing will have altered. The directors would not work less satisfactorily for society than for shareholders.

We must distinguish between two groups of joint-stock companies and similar concerns. In the first group, consisting for the large part of smaller companies, a few individuals unite in a common enterprise in the legal form of a company. They are often the heirs of the founders of the company, or often previous competitors who have amalgamated. Here the actual control and management of business is in the hands of the shareholders themselves or at least of some of the shareholders, who do business in their own interest; or in that of closely related shareholders such as wives, minors, etc. The directors in their capacity as members of the board of management or of the board of control, and sometimes also in an attenuated legal capacity, themselves exercise the decisive influence in the conduct of affairs. Nor is this affected by the circumstance that sometimes part of the share-capital is held by a financial consortium or bank.

---

57 Cf. Preliminary Report of the Socialization Commission on the Issue of the Socialization of Coal Mining, concluded 15th February, 1919 (Berlin, 1919), p. 13th

Here in fact the company is only differentiated from the public commercial company by its legal form.

The situation is quite different in the case of large-scale companies, where only a fraction of the shareholders, i.e. the big shareholders, participate in the actual control of the enterprise. And these usually have the same interest in the firm's prosperity as any property holder. Still, it may well be that they have interests other than those of the vast majority of small shareholders, who are excluded from the management even if they own the larger part of the share-capital. Severe collisions may occur, when the firm's business is so handled on behalf of the directors that the shareholders are injured. But be that as it may, it is clear that the real holders of power in companies run the business in their own interest, whether it coincides with that of the shareholders or not. In the long run it will generally be to the advantage of the solid company administrator, who is not merely bent on making a transient profit, to represent the shareholders' interests only in every case and to avoid manipulations which might damage them. This holds good in the first instance for banks and financial groups, which should not trifle at the public's expense with the credit they enjoy. Thus it is not merely on the prescriptiveness of ethical motives that the success of companies depends.

The situation is completely transformed when an undertaking is nationalized. The motive force disappears with the exclusion of the material interests of private individuals, and if State and municipal enterprises thrive at all, they owe it to the taking over of "management" from private enterprise, or to the fact that they are ever driven to reforms and innovations by the business men from whom they purchase their instruments of production and raw material.

Since we are in a position to survey decades of State and socialist endeavor, it is now generally recognized that there is no internal pressure to reform and improvement of production in socialist undertakings, that they cannot be adjusted to the changing conditions of demand, and that in a word they are a dead limb in the economic organism. All attempts to breathe life into them have so far been in vain. It was supposed that a reform in the system of remuneration might achieve the desired end. If the managers of these enterprises were interested in the yield, it was thought they would be in a position comparable to that of the manager of large-scale companies. This is a fatal error. The managers of large-scale companies are bound up with the interests of the businesses they administer in an entirely different way from what could be the case in public concerns. They are either already owners of a not inconsiderable fraction of the share capital, or hope to become so in due course. Further, they are in a position to obtain profits by stock exchange speculation in the company's shares. They have the prospect of bequeathing their positions to, or at least securing part of their influence for, their heirs. The type to which the success of joint-stock companies is to be attributed, is not that of a complacently prosperous managing director resembling the civil servant in his outlook and experience; rather it is precisely the manager, promoter, and man of affairs, who is himself interested as a shareholder, whom it is the aim of all nationalization and municipalization to exclude.

It is not generally legitimate to appeal in a socialist context to such arguments in order to ensure the success of an economic order built on socialist foundations. All socialist systems, including that of Karl Marx, and his orthodox supporters, proceed from the assumption that in a socialist society a conflict between the interests of the particular and general could not possibly arise. Everybody will act in his own interest in giving of his best because he participates in the product of all economic activity. The obvious objection that the individual is very little concerned whether he himself is diligent and enthusiastic, and that it is of greater moment to him that everybody else should be, is either completely ignored or is insufficiently dealt with by them. They believe they can construct a socialist commonwealth on the basis of the Categorical Imperative alone. How lightly it is their wont to proceed in this way is best shown by Kautsky when he says, "If socialism is a social necessity, then it would be human nature and not socialism which would have to readjust itself, if ever the two clashed."[58] This is nothing but sheer Utopianism.

But even if we for the moment grant that these Utopian expectations can actually be realized, that each individual in a socialist society will exert himself with the same zeal as he does today in a society where he is subjected to the pressure of free competition, there still remains the problem of measuring the result of economic activity in a socialist commonwealth which does not permit of any economic calculation. We cannot act economically if we are not in a position to understand economizing.

A popular slogan affirms that if we think less bureaucratically and more commercially in communal enterprises, they will work

58 Cf. Karl Kautsky, Preface to "Atlanticus" [Gustav Jaeckh], *Produktion und Konsum im Sozialstaat* (Stuttgart: J.H.W. Dietz, 1898), p. 14.

just as well as private enterprises. The leading positions must be occupied by merchants, and then income will grow apace. Unfortunately "commercial-mindedness" is not something external, which can be arbitrarily transferred. A merchant's qualities are not the property of a person depending on inborn aptitude, nor are they acquired by studies in a commercial school or by working in a commercial house, or even by having been a businessman oneself for some period of time. The entrepreneur's commercial attitude and activity arises from his position in the economic process and is lost with its disappearance. When a successful business man is appointed the manager of a public enterprise, he may still bring with him certain experiences from his previous occupation, and be able to turn them to good account in a routine fashion for some time. Still, with his entry into communal activity he ceases to be a merchant and becomes as much a bureaucrat as any other placeman in the public employ. It is not a knowledge of bookkeeping, of business organization, or of the style of commercial correspondence, or even a dispensation from a commercial high school, which makes the merchant, but his characteristic position in the production process, which allows of the identification of the firm's and his own interests. It is no solution of the problem when Otto Bauer in his most recently published work proposes that the directors of the National Central Bank, on whom leadership in the economic process will be conferred, should be nominated by a Collegium, to which representatives of the teaching staff of the commercial high schools would also belong[59]. Like Plato's

59 Cf. Otto Bauer, *Der Weg zum Sozialismus* (Vienna: Ignaz Brand, 1919), p. 25.

philosophers, the directors so appointed may well be the wisest and best of their kind, but they cannot be merchants in their posts as leaders of a socialist society, even if they should have been previously.

It is a general complaint that the administration of public undertakings lacks initiative. It is believed that this might be remedied by changes in organization. This also is a grievous mistake. The management of a socialist concern cannot entirely be placed in the hands of a single individual, because there must always be the suspicion that he will permit errors inflicting heavy damages on the community. But if the important conclusions are made dependent on the votes of committees, or on the consent of the relevant government offices, then limitations are imposed on the individual's initiative. Committees are rarely inclined to introduce bold innovations. The lack of free initiative in public business rests not on an absence of organization, it is inherent in the nature of the business itself. One cannot transfer free disposal of the factors of production to an employee, however high his rank, and this becomes even less possible, the more strongly he is materially interested in the successful performance of his duties; for in practice the propertyless manager can only be held morally responsible for losses incurred. And so ethical losses are juxtaposed with opportunities for material gain. The property owner on the other hand himself bears responsibility, as he himself must primarily feel the loss arising from unwisely conducted business. It is precisely in this that there is a characteristic difference between liberal and socialist production.

5. The Most Recent Socialist Doctrines and the Problem of Economic Calculation

Since recent events helped socialist parties to obtain power in Russia, Hungary, Germany and Austria, and have thus made the execution of a socialist nationalization program a topical issue,[60] Marxist writers have themselves begun to deal more closely with the problems of the regulation of the socialist commonwealth. But even now they still cautiously avoid the crucial question, leaving it to be tackled by the despised "Utopians." They themselves prefer to confine their attention to what is to be done in the immediate future; they are forever drawing up programs of the path to Socialism and not of Socialism itself. The only possible conclusion from all these writings is that they are not even conscious of the larger problem of economic calculation in a socialist society.

To Otto Bauer the nationalization of the banks appears the final and decisive step in the carrying through of the socialist nationalization program. If all banks are nationalized and amalgamated into a single central bank, then its administrative board becomes "the supreme economic authority, the chief administrative organ of the whole economy. Only by nationalization of the banks does society obtain the power to regulate its labor according to a plan, and to distribute its resources rationally among the various branches of production, so as to adapt them to the nation's needs."[61] Bauer is

---

60 [The reader will remember that Mises is writing in 1920.]

61 Cf. Otto Bauer, *Der Weg zum Sozialismus* (Vienna: Ignaz Brand, 1919), p. 26 f.

not discussing the monetary arrangements which will prevail in the socialist commonwealth after the completion of the nationalization of the banks. Like other Marxists he is trying to show how simply and obviously the future socialist order of society will evolve from the conditions prevailing in a developed capitalist economy. "It suffices to transfer to the nation's representatives the power now exercised by bank shareholders through the Administrative Boards they elect,"[62] in order to socialize the banks and thus to lay the last brick on the edifice of socialism. Bauer leaves his readers completely ignorant of the fact that the nature of the banks is entirely changed in the process of nationalization and amalgamation into one central bank. Once the banks merge into a single bank, their essence is wholly transformed; they are then in a position to issue credit without any limitation.[63] In this fashion the monetary system as we know it today disappears of itself. When in addition the single central bank is nationalized in a society, which is otherwise already completely socialized, market dealings disappear and all exchange transactions are abolished. At the same time the Bank ceases to be a bank, its specific functions are extinguished, for there is no longer any place for it in such a society. It may be that the name "Bank" is retained, that the Supreme Economic Council of the socialist community is called the Board of Directors of the Bank,

---

62 Cf. Otto Bauer, *Der Weg zum Sozialismus* (Vienna: Ignaz Brand, 1919), p. 25.

63 Cf. Ludwig von Mises, *Theorie des Geldes und der Umlaufsmittel* (Munich and Leipzig: Duncker & Humblot, 1912), p. 474 ff. [See the English translation by H.E. Batson, *The Theory of Money and Credit* (Indianapolis: Liberty Classics, 1980), [Compare p. 411 of the 1980 English edition.]

and that they hold their meetings in a building formerly occupied by a bank. But it is no longer a bank, it fulfils none of those functions which a bank fulfils in an economic system resting on the private ownership of the means of production and the use of a general medium of exchange—money. It no longer distributes any credit, for a socialist society makes credit of necessity impossible. Bauer himself does not tell us what a bank is, but he begins his chapter on the nationalization of the banks with the sentence: "All disposable capital flows into a common pool in the banks."[64] As a Marxist must he not raise the question of what the banks' activities will be after the abolition of capitalism?

All other writers who have grappled with the problems of the organization of the socialist commonwealth are guilty of similar confusions. They do not realize that the bases of economic calculation are removed by the exclusion of exchange and the pricing mechanism, and that something must be substituted in its place, if all economy is not to be abolished and a hopeless chaos is not to result. People believe that socialist institutions might evolve without further ado from those of a capitalist economy. This is not at all the case. And it becomes all the more grotesque when we talk of banks, banks management, etc. in a socialist commonwealth.

Reference to the conditions that have developed in Russia and Hungary under Soviet rule proves nothing. What we have there is nothing but a picture of the destruction of an existing order of social production, for which a closed peasant household economy

64 Cf. Otto Bauer, *Der Weg zum Sozialismus* (Vienna: Ignaz Brand, 1919), p. 24 f.

has been substituted. All branches of production depending on social division of labor are in a state of entire dissolution. What is happening under the rule of Lenin and Trotsky is merely destruction and annihilation. Whether, as the liberals[65] hold, socialism must inevitably draw these consequences in its train, or whether, as the socialists retort, this is only a result of the fact that the Soviet Republic is attacked from without, is a question of no interest to us in this context. All that has to be established is the fact that the Soviet socialist commonwealth has not even begun to discuss the problem of economic calculation, nor has it any cause to do so. For where things are still produced for the market in Soviet Russia in spite of governmental prohibitions, they are valued in terms of money, for there exists to that extent private ownership of the means of production, and goods are sold against money. Even the Government cannot deny the necessity, which it confirms by increasing the amount of money in circulation, of retaining a monetary system for at least the transition period.

That the essence of the problem to be faced has not yet come to light in Soviet Russia, Lenin's statements in his essay on *Die nächsten Aufgaben der Sowjetmacht* best show. In the dictator's deliberations there ever recurs the thought that the immediate and most pressing task of Russian communism is "the organization of bookkeeping and control of those concerns, in which the capitalists have already been expropriated, and of all other

65 [Mises is using the term "liberal" here in its nineteenth-century European sense, meaning "classical liberal" or libertarian. On liberalism see Mises' *Liberalism: In the Classical Tradition*, translated by Ralph Raico (Irvington-on-Hudson, N.Y.: Foundation for Economic Education, 1985).]

economic concerns."[66] Even so Lenin is far from realizing that an entirely new problem is here involved which it is impossible to solve with the conceptual instruments of "bourgeois" culture. Like a real politician, he does not bother with issues beyond his nose. He still finds himself surrounded by monetary transactions, and does not notice that with progressive socialization money also necessarily loses its function as the medium of exchange in general use, to the extent that private property and with it exchange disappear. The implication of Lenin's reflections is that he would like to re-introduce into Soviet business "bourgeois" bookkeeping carried on on a monetary basis. Therefore he also desires to restore "bourgeois experts" to a state of grace.[67] For the rest Lenin is as little aware as Bauer of the fact that in a socialist commonwealth the functions of the bank are unthinkable in their existing sense. He wishes to go farther with the "nationalization of the banks" and to proceed" to a transformation of the banks into the nodal point of social bookkeeping under socialism."[68]

Lenin's ideas on the socialist economic system, to which he is striving to lead his people, are generally obscure.

66 Cf. V.I. Lenin, *Die nächsten Aufgaben der Sowjetmacht (Berlin: Wilmersdorf*, 1919), pp. 12 f., 22ff. [English translation, The Soviets at Work—This edition.]

67 Cf. V.I. Lenin, *Die nächsten Aufgaben der Sowjetmacht* (Berlin: Wilmersdorf, 1919), pp. 15. [English translation, The Soviets at Work—This edition.]

68 Cf. V.I. Lenin, *Die nächsten Aufgaben der Sowjetmacht* (Berlin: Wilmersdorf, 1919), pp. 21 and 26. [English translation, The Soviets at Work—This edition.] Compare also Bukharin, Das Programm der Kommunisten (Zürich: no pub., 1918), pp. 27 ff.

> "The socialist state," he says "can only arise as a net of producing and consuming communes, which conscientiously record their production and consumption, go about their labour economically, uninterruptedly raise their labour productivity and thus attain the possibility of lowering the working day to seven or six hours or even lower."[69] "Every factor, every village appears as a production and consumption commune having the right and obligation to apply the general Soviet legislation in its own way ('in its own way' not in the sense of its violation but in the sense of the variety of its forms of realisation), and to solve in its own way the problems of calculating the production and distribution of products."[70]

"The chief communes must and will serve the most backward ones as educators, teachers, and stimulating leaders." The successes of the chief communes must be broadcast in all their details in order to provide a good example. The communes "showing good business results" should be immediately rewarded "by a curtailment of the working day and with an increase in wages, and by allowing more attention to be paid to cultural and

69 Cf. V.I. Lenin, *Die nächsten Aufgaben der Sowjetmacht* (Berlin: Wilmersdorf, 1919), pp. 24 f.. [English translation, The Soviets at Work—This edition.]

70 Cf. V.I. Lenin, *Die nächsten Aufgaben der Sowjetmacht* (Berlin: Wilmersdorf, 1919), pp. 32. [English translation, The Soviets at Work—This edition.]

aesthetic goods and values."[71]

We can infer that Lenin's ideal is a state of society in which the means of production are not the property of a few districts, municipalities, or even of the workers in the concern, but of the whole community. His ideal is socialist and not syndicalist. This need not be specially stressed for a Marxist such as Lenin. It is not extraordinary of Lenin the theorist, but of Lenin the statesman, who is the leader of the syndicalist and small-holding peasant Russian revolution. However, at the moment we are engaged with the writer Lenin and may consider his ideals separately, without letting ourselves be disturbed by the picture of sober reality. According to Lenin the theorist, every large agricultural and industrial concern is a member of the great commonwealth of labor. Those who are active in this commonwealth have the right of self-government; they exercise a profound influence on the direction of production and again on the distribution of the goods they are assigned for consumption. Still labor is the property of the whole society, and as its product belongs to society also, it therefore disposes of its distribution. How, we must now ask, is calculation in the economy carried on in a socialist commonwealth which is so organized? Lenin gives us a most inadequate answer by referring us back to statistics.

> We must bring statistics to the masses, make it popular, so that the active population will gradually learn by themselves

71 Cf. V.I. Lenin, *Die nächsten Aufgaben der Sowjetmacht* (Berlin: Wilmersdorf, 1919), pp. 33. [English translation, The Soviets at Work—This edition.]

> to understand and realize how much and what kind of work must be done, how much and what kind of recreation should be taken, so that the comparison of the economy's industrial results in the case of individual communes becomes the object of general interest and education.[72]

From these scanty allusions it is impossible to infer what Lenin understands by statistics and whether he is thinking of monetary or *in natura* computation. In any case, we must refer back to what we have said about the impossibility of learning the money prices of production-goods in a socialist commonwealth and about the difficulties standing in the way of *in natura* valuation.[73] Statistics would only be applicable to economic calculation if it could go beyond the *in natura* calculation, whose ill-suitedness for this purpose we have demonstrated. It is naturally impossible where no exchange relations are formed between goods in the process of trade.

---

72 Cf. V.I. Lenin, *Die nächsten Aufgaben der Sowjetmacht* (Berlin: Wilmersdorf, 1919), pp. 33. [English translation, The Soviets at Work—This edition.]

73 Neurath, too, imputes great importance to statistics for the setting up of the socialist economic plan. Otto Neurath (Durch die Kriegswirtschaft zur Naturalwirtschaft [Munich: G.D.W. Callwey, 1919], pp. 212 et seq.).

THE FUTURE OF LIBERALISM

This is an excerpt from Mises's book, originally published in 1927 as *Liberalismus* [English: *Liberalism*] (Liberalismus. Jena: Gustav Fischer, 1927). The first English translation was published 1962 as *The Free and Prosperous Commonwealth* (NY: D. Van Nostrand, 1962)

All earlier civilizations perished, or at least reached a state of stagnation, long before they had attained the level of material development that modern European civilization has succeeded in achieving. Nations were destroyed by wars with foreign enemies as well as by internecine strife. Anarchy forced a retrogression in the division of labor; cities, commerce, and industry declined; and, with the decay of their economic foundations, intellectual and moral refinements had to give way to ignorance and brutality. The Europeans of the modern age have succeeded in intensifying the social bonds among individuals and nations much more strongly than was ever the case before in history. This was an achievement of the ideology of liberalism, which, from the end of the seventeenth century, was elaborated with ever increasing clarity and precision and continually gained in influence over men's minds. Liberalism and capitalism created the foundations on which are based all the marvels characteristic of our modern way of life.

Now our civilization is beginning to scent a whiff of death in the air. Dilettantes loudly proclaim that all civilizations, including our own, must perish: this is an inexorable law. Europe's final hour has come, warn these prophets of doom, and they find credence. An autumnal mood is perceptibly beginning to set in everywhere.

But modem civilization will not perish unless it does so by its own act of self-destruction. No external enemy can destroy it the way the Spaniards once destroyed the civilization of the Aztecs, for no one on earth can match his strength against the standard-bearers of modern civilization. Only inner enemies can threaten it. It can come to an end only if the ideas of liberalism are supplanted by an antiliberal ideology hostile to social cooperation.

There has come to be a growing realization that material progress is possible only in a liberal, capitalist society. Even if this point is not expressly conceded by the antiliberal, it is fully acknowledged indirectly in the panegyrics extolling the idea of stability and a state of rest. The material advances of recent generations, it is said, have, of course, been really very agreeable and beneficial. Now, however, it is time to call a halt. The frantic hustle and bustle of modern capitalism must make way for tranquil contemplation. One must acquire time for self-communion, and so another economic system must take the place of capitalism, one that is not always restlessly chasing after novelties and innovations. The romantic looks back nostalgically to the economic conditions of the Middle Ages – not to the Middle Ages as they actually were, but to an image of them constructed by his fancy without any counterpart in historical reality. Or he turns his gaze upon the Orient – again not, of course, the real Orient, but a dream-vision of his phantasm. How happy men were without modern technology and modern culture. How could we ever have renounced this paradise so light-mindedly?

Whoever preaches the return to simple forms of the economic organization of society ought to keep in mind that only our type of economic system offers the possibility of supporting in the style to which we have become accustomed today the number of people who now populate the earth. A return to the Middle Ages means the extermination of many hundreds of millions of people. The friends of stability and rest, it is true, say that one by no means has to go as far as that. It suffices to hold fast to what has already been achieved and to forgo further advances.

Those who extol the state of rest and stable equilibrium forget that there is in man, in so far as he is a thinking being, an inherent desire for the improvement of his material condition. This impulse cannot be eradicated; it is the motive power of all human action. If one prevents a man from working for the good of society while at the same time providing for the satisfaction of his own needs, then only one way remains open to him: to make himself richer and others poorer by the violent oppression and spoliation of his fellow men.

It is true that all this straining and struggling to increase their standard of living does not make men any happier. Nevertheless, it is in the nature of man continually to strive for an improvement in his material condition. If he is forbidden the satisfaction of this aspiration, he becomes dull and brutish. The masses will not listen to exhortations to be moderate and contented; it may be that the philosophers who preach such admonitions are laboring under a serious self-delusion. If one tells people that their fathers had it much worse, they answer that they do not know why they should not have it still better.

Now, whether it is good or bad, whether it receives the sanction of the moral censor or not, it is certain that men always strive for an improvement in their conditions and always will. This is man's inescapable destiny. The restlessness and inquietude of modern man is a stirring of the mind, the nerves, and the senses. One can as easily restore to him the innocence of childhood as lead him back to the passivity of past periods of human history.

But, after all, what is being offered in return for the renunciation of further material progress? Happiness and contentment, inner harmony and peace will not be created simply because people are no longer intent on further improvement in the satisfaction of their needs. Soured by resentment, the literati imagine that poverty and the absence of wants create especially favorable conditions for the development of man's spiritual capacities, but this is nonsense. In discussing these questions, one should avoid euphemisms and call things by their right names. Modern wealth expresses itself above all in the cult of the body: hygiene, cleanliness, sport. Today still the luxury of the well-to-do - no longer, perhaps, in the United States, but everywhere else - these will come within the reach of everyone in the not too distant future if economic development progresses as it has hitherto. Is it thought that man's inner life is in any way furthered by excluding the masses from the attainment of the level of physical culture that the well-to-do already enjoy? Is happiness to be found in the unkempt body?

To the panegyrists of the Middle Ages one can only answer that we know nothing about whether the medieval man felt happier than the modern man. But we may leave it to those who hold up the mode of life of the Orientals as a model for us to answer the question whether Asia is really the paradise that they describe it as.

The fulsome praise of the stationary economy as a social ideal is the last remaining argument that the enemies of liberalism have to fall back upon in order to justify their doctrines. Let us keep clearly in mind, however, that the starting-point of their critique was that liberalism and capitalism impede the development of productive forces, that they are responsible for the poverty of the masses. The opponents of liberalism have alleged that what they are aiming at is a social order that could create more wealth than the one they are attacking. And now, driven to the wall by the counterattack of economics and sociology, they must concede that only capitalism and liberalism, only private property and the unhampered activity of entrepreneurs, can guarantee the highest productivity of human labor.

It is often maintained that what divides present-day political parties is a basic opposition in their ultimate philosophical commitments that cannot be settled by rational argument. The discussion of these antagonisms must therefore necessarily prove fruitless. Each side will remain unshaken in its conviction because the latter is based on a comprehensive worldview that cannot be altered by any considerations proposed by the reason. The ultimate ends toward which men strive are diverse. Hence, it is altogether out of the question that men aiming at these diverse ends could agree on a uniform procedure.

Nothing is more absurd than this belief. .... The political antagonisms of today are not controversies over ultimate questions of philosophy, but opposing answers to the question how a goal that all acknowledge as legitimate can be achieved most quickly and with the least sacrifice. This goal, at which all men aim, is the best possible satisfaction of human wants; it is prosperity and abundance. Of course, this is not all that men aspire to, but it is all that they can expect to attain by resort to external means and by way of social cooperation. The inner blessings—happiness, peace of mind, exaltation—must be sought by each man within himself alone.

Liberalism is no religion, no world view, no party of special interests. It is no religion because it demands neither faith nor devotion, because there is nothing mystical about it, and because it has no dogmas. It is no world view because it does not try to explain the cosmos and because it says nothing and does not seek to say anything about the meaning and purpose of human existence. It is no party of special interests because it does not provide or seek to provide any special advantage whatsoever to any individual or any group. It is something entirely different. It is an ideology, a doctrine of the mutual relationship among the members of society and, at the same time, the application of this doctrine to the conduct of men in actual society. It promises nothing that exceeds what can be accomplished in society and through society. It seeks to give men only one thing, the peaceful, undisturbed development of material well-being for all, in order thereby to shield them from the external causes of pain and suffering as far as it lies within the power of social institutions to do so at all. To diminish suffering, to increase happiness: that is its aim.

No sect and no political party has believed that it could afford to forgo advancing its cause by appealing to men's senses. Rhetorical bombast, music and song resound, banners wave, flowers and colors serve as symbols, and the leaders seek to attach their followers to their own person. Liberalism has nothing to do with all this. It has no party flower and no party color, no party song and no party idols, no symbols and no slogans. It has the substance and the arguments. These must lead it to victory.

ABOUT THE AUTHOR

Ludwig Heinrich Edler von Mises (1881-1973) was an economist, historian, and philosopher. Mises wrote and lectured extensively on behalf of the market order and is best known for his 1949 book *Human Action*. Mises worked and taught in Vienna until he was driven out by the Nazi movement in 1934. He took sanctuary in Geneva until 1940, immigrated to the United States, and eventually taught at New York University. Mises's colleague Friedrich Hayek viewed Mises as one of the major figures in the revival of liberalism in the post-war era. Mises's Private Seminar in Vienna was a formative event for many social scientists of the period, and many of its alumni, including Hayek and Oskar Morgenstern, emigrated from Austria to the United States and Great Britain.

ABOUT AIER

The American Institute for Economic Research in Great Barrington, Massachusetts, was founded in 1933 as the first independent voice for sound economics in the United States. Today it publishes ongoing research, hosts educational programs, publishes books, sponsors interns and scholars, and is home to the world-renowned Bastiat Society and the highly respected Sound Money Project. The American Institute for Economic Research is a 501c3 public charity.

INDEX

Made in United States
North Haven, CT
07 March 2026

89587899R00146